WOMEN'S SPIRITUAL PASSAGES

Women's
SPIRITUAL
PASSAGES
Celebrating Faith after 40

Edited by Lucinda Secrest McDowell

Harold Shaw Publishers
Wheaton, Illinois

ISBN 0-87788-456-0

Cover design by David LaPlaca
Edited by Cathy Walker and Mary Horner Collins

Library of Congress Cataloging in Publication Data

Women's Spiritual passages : celebrating faith after 40 / edited by Lucinda
    Secrest McDowell.
      ISBN 0-87788-456-0
      1. Middle aged women--Religious life. 2. Spiritual life--Christianity.
    I. McDowell, Lucinda Secrest, 1953-
    BV4579.5.K44 1996
    277.3'0825'082—dc20   95-44698

---

02 01 00 99 98 97 96

10 9 8 7 6 5 4 3 2 1

For my friends
(you know who you are),

those who have touched me in so many ways,
thereby becoming the beautiful threads in
the tapestry that is my life.

Thank you for loving me, accepting me,
and encouraging me to greater challenges!

Contents

Acknowledgments

Writing this book has been a joy and a privilege. I like nothing better than introducing people to other people, knowing how much they will gain from one another. So, in *Women's Spiritual Passages* I am sharing with you the remarkable women whom God has placed in my path through the years. I am excited to introduce them to you, for they have truly made my life richer.

This project was not accomplished alone. I have many people to thank, but can only list a few:

My parents, Pratt and Sarah Secrest, who provided a strong foundation of love and encouragement for me, which has certainly helped me be able to celebrate the faith after forty.

My husband, Michael McDowell, who has graciously kept faith with me.

My children, Justin, Timothy, Fiona, and Margaret Sarah, who are very relieved that this book is finally finished and Mama can "cook better meals and clean the house."

My two forty-something sisters, Cathy Secrest Ray and Susan Secrest Waters, who have prayed for me and taught me more than they'll ever know.

My kindred-spirit friend, Marjorie Wallem Rowe, who has prayed for and encouraged me in this project in more ways than I can recall.

All the contributing authors—we would not have a book without your willingness to be real in a redemptive way. Thank you for risking involvement—may you see much fruit.

My friend, Faith Curtis, who, among other things, painstakingly typed at least half of these stories when I was running out of time.

My neighbor and friend, Jane Benard, who patiently helped me in many a computer crisis (every author should have a resident computer expert living next door).

Friends Joyce Mattison and Jocelyn Bagger, who helped with typing and mailings to this extended list of contributors.

Numerous friends such as Grace, Cindy, Kathi, Dana, Terri, Kathy, Judy, Peggy, Arlene, Kay, and Sally (and many more, but I can't name them all, sorry), who prayed and also provided childcare, meals, gardening, and "taxi service" on the days I was stuck in my attic chained to the computer.

My editor at Harold Shaw Publishers, Mary Horner Collins, who believed in me and this project from the very beginning. Thank you, Mary. I hope this is a good fortieth birthday present for you.

My Lord and Savior Jesus Christ, who has been *utterly faithful* through all the days of my life. "My times are in thy hands, Lord."

Introduction

Each passage of life brings unexpected choices and challenges. This is especially true of baby-boomer Christians—those women who began their journey of faith during the turbulent 1960s and 1970s. What's happened to them? Did they fulfill their dreams, or just give in to the system? Was it really possible to "have it all"—career, family, marriage, and ministry? Did their faith survive the self-examination and recovery process of the 1980s? How have the passages of life changed them? And what new risks lie ahead for the second part of life?

Last summer I picked up *Clarity* magazine and read these words by author Beth Spring: "As the baby-boom generation hits midlife, a natural process of reassessment, reflection and at times radical change in direction occurs. Their growing interest in all things spiritual presents new opportunities for God to speak; it also hastens the arrival of subtle and not-so-subtle alternatives not centered on Jesus."

Today another publication, *Next*, arrived in the mail with this thought: "Are we in a period of reassessing where we have been and more importantly, where we want to go? Are we collectively acknowledging what many are individually discovering, . . . that success and achievement are not substitutes for significance and meaning?"

Most experts agree that midlife is a time of taking inventory—looking back and also looking ahead. The women in this book, having reached the age of forty, are now looking at their lives and reflecting on the lessons they've learned. Their candid stories revolve around five areas of spiritual passage common to most of us: becoming "real" and more honest with ourselves, weathering the storms of life, making choices and learning to live with them, grieving our losses, and investing in the future of our children and others.

A few months before my fortieth birthday I, too, felt a strong urge to make such an evaluation. I decided to treat myself to a trip to California for the twenty-fourth annual Mt. Hermon Christian Writers Conference. The advanced writers track gave me lots of insight and honing of my craft, but I also skipped a few sessions. I was determined to spend time alone with the Lord, hoping to receive direction on a number of fronts—my family, vocation, and my writing career.

One of the first things I was urged to do was to write a "mission statement" for my life. I don't know why I had never done this before, because it's a great idea. After writing it, I pledged to put every opportunity that came my way through this filter—if it wasn't part of my life's mission, it was expendable.

> "My mission is to glorify God and live in His grace and freedom, and through the power of the Holy Spirit, to use my gifts to communicate God's faithfulness, extend His grace, and encourage others to trust Him fully."

The next day I was totally flabbergasted to be announced as the recipient of the "Writer of the Year" award. To me, this was a confirmation from the Lord that perhaps I did have a contribution to make in that field. I returned home to Connecticut, my husband, and four children and promptly experienced writer's block for six months!

Since I wasn't able to write, I had a lot of time to think. I remembered that every night at the conference the speaker had closed with this prayer by Brennan Manning:

May all your expectations be frustrated.
May all your plans be thwarted.
May all your desires be withered into nothingness.
That you may experience the powerlessness and poverty of a child, . . . and sing and dance in the compassion of God who is Father, Son and Spirit. Amen.

What a great reminder of the source of all creativity and joy! I had faced many frustrations and thwarted plans. But out of that year came my first book *Amazed By Grace*, in which I chronicled all the spiritual lessons and discoveries of grace I had experienced in my first forty years.

Everyone goes through times of rethinking their faith and considering their spiritual passages. Everyone also has a story to tell. The problem is, the older we get, the fewer the people who want to hear our stories. (Unless we're one hundred years old, then we've got a real best-seller!) But as I thought of the myriad of folk who had touched my life through the years, I realized what treasure there was in their faith journeys. So like the old movies where Judy Garland and Mickey Rooney "gathered all their friends together to do a show," I decided to gather all my friends together to do a book!

Well, not *all* my friends, but at least the ones who had recently turned forty. Some of them I met in college or seminary, some are former colleagues from my various jobs around the world, while others are folk I met in the most unexpected places and immediately connected with on more than a surface level. What a variety of people!

Most of these women made faith commitments early in life. They live all over the United States and Canada, plus South America, Eastern Europe, Asia, and Africa. They are white and black, married, single, divorced, and widowed. They are mothers, aunts, stepmothers, and yes, even grandmothers (at forty). Most are college graduates, several have their doctorates, and many earned master's degrees. There are Presbyterians, Congregationalists, Episcopalians, Baptists, Charismatics, Methodists, Anglicans, Lutherans, and more.

All are women in leadership—as Bible teachers, homemakers, professional clergy, counselors, speakers, missionaries, professors, musicians, administrators, and authors.

And all participants, including yours truly, are self-proclaimed sinners-saved-by-grace. They are a courageous lot. Each of the women you will meet on the following pages has dug deep to share from her heart some of the hard lessons in life.

Why go to all the bother of gathering and putting together fifty stories from relatively unknown forty-something women?

So you could read what God is doing today in women just like you. Women who have made the powerful and highly intelligent choice to claim Jesus as Lord of their lives for the long haul. Each of them had other options—some more lucrative, glamorous, or comfortable—but they have kept the faith into midlife.

We are rapidly becoming a nation of midlifers. As I was preparing a surprise scrapbook for my husband's fiftieth birthday this summer, I came across this statistic: "Beginning January 1, 1996, every eight seconds, and continuing for the next eighteen years, someone in the United States will turn 50." That's us, folks. And while many books on midlife seem to dwell on the negative (or how to pretend you *aren't* forty-plus), this book is decidedly different. I asked each woman, *"What is the best part of being forty-plus years old?"* Their answers may surprise you. These women make forty sound terrific!

So, if you're not yet forty, by the time you finish this, you'll want to be. Join me on this great adventure of savoring the stories. Laugh, cry, and reminisce with women just like you who never thought their lives would end up this way, but who celebrate with joy the sovereignty and serendipity of God.

Lucinda Secrest McDowell
"Gracehaven"
Wethersfield, Connecticut

I. BECOMING REAL

The purple ink on the envelope loudly advertised "Exciting Info for Your 20th Reunion This Year!" My immediate reaction was, *It can't be! Surely twenty years haven't passed since I graduated from Furman University. Why, it seems just like yesterday; maybe they mean my tenth reunion.* Then I remembered attending my fifteenth reunion with a nursing baby who is now in kindergarten. "I can't believe it!" I shouted to an empty house. Then I sat down as it sank in. "I am middle-aged," I admitted softly. "This year I turned forty-one and sent a son off to college. Now I'm the age my folks were when I was in college. No, surely they were older. Weren't they?"

I opened the letter and noted the date of the reunion. I couldn't go due to speaking engagements. In a way, I was relieved. After all, those twenty years have left their mark on me. Ouch. Am I really that vain?

I decided to fill out and return a questionnaire even though I'd be absent. Truly inane questions like, "What was your best date at Furman? Your worst date?" Then a real doozy—"What was the best lie you told your parents in 1974?" Now that gave me pause. I didn't want to write in the truth, that I *didn't* lie to my parents. Talk about seeming like a goody two-shoes (bad enough I was married to a minister now . . .). But the fact is I didn't lie. Or did I?

Picking up my pen, I carefully filled in the line with my honest answer to the question, "What was the best lie you told your parents in 1974?"

"Everything's just fine!"

Everything was not always "just fine" back in 1974, and it still isn't always in 1994. The difference is me. Had it really taken twenty years for me to become real enough to face pain, admit failure, and show need?

I grew up deeply entrenched in what Pat Conroy refers to in *The Prince of Tides* as "the Southern way." We don't talk about life's unpleasantness. We offer a poised and pretty face to the world and push the bad deep inside—a "steel magnolia" if you please. But how often have I felt just like M'Lynn in the movie *Steel Magnolias* as she walks out of the cemetery after burying her daughter: "I'm fine, I'm fine, I'm fine! No, I'm not—I just want to hit someone so hard until they hurt as much as I do! No, . . . I'll be fine."

It took me a long time to learn how to live in God's grace. To truly believe that God's love for me is unconditional and I can't earn it or lose it. But in my forties, I've finally become free. I have learned how to face life head-on—the defeats as well as the victories, the brokenness as well as the strength.

Brennan Manning related a similar discovery in his book *Abba's Child*. He writes, "The longer you spend time in the presence of Jesus, the more accustomed you grow to His face, the less adulation you will need because you have discovered for yourself that He is Enough. And in the Presence, you will delight in the discovery of what it means to live by grace and not by performance."

Recently a woman from my Bible study approached me in the church parking lot and gave me what I think was a genuine compliment: "Cindy, I love your Bible teaching because you're not like any other minister's wife I've ever known. I mean, you're just like us, you don't have it all together and you say so. And I loved it when you shared about that time you were speaking and your front-clasp bra came unclasped. I know that sounds funny, but I knew right then that if God loves and can use somebody like you, he probably loves me, too."

Hmmmm.

My hardcover inscribed copy of the Margery Williams classic *The Velveteen Rabbit* was given to me in my college years. At that time, it had almost become a cult book among the youth. Ours was a generation that desperately wanted to be "real," which is also what the velveteen rabbit desired. We didn't want to just sit on a shelf presenting a perfect, plastic face to the world. We wanted to experience life to the fullest.

We thought that if we said, sang, and wore everything different from our parents' generation, then we would be real and less hypocritical. So we spent a lot of time and energy bucking the system and conforming to that ideal persona—the nonconformist. But even that didn't make us real, only frustrated.

It took time. It took life. We had to experience dismal failure and marvelous success—and learn how to handle both with integrity. Sometimes we had to dig deep to finally face up to old wounds and ugly pain. But in the healing process we felt stronger and ready to forge ahead. We experimented with relationships, vocation, and spirituality.

The results taught us about what is truly important. We had children, buried parents, and fought to keep our marriage vows.

In the midst of all this, we became very much like the velveteen rabbit, who was "so happy that he never noticed how his beautiful velveteen fur was getting shabbier and shabbier, and his tail coming unsewn, and all the pink rubbed off his nose." Our battle scars told it all—the years had taken their toll. But there was certainly more to being real than just looking all beat up.

We had to be unconditionally loved.

God's love had been there for us all along, but it took different things for each of us to finally accept it. The velveteen rabbit's friend, the Skin Horse, explains it best:

> Real isn't how you are made. . . . It's a thing that happens to you. It doesn't happen all at once. . . . You become. It takes a long time. That's why it doesn't often happen to people who break easily, or who have sharp edges, or who have to be carefully kept. Generally, by the time you are Real, most of your hair has been loved off, and your eyes drop out and you get loose in the joints and very shabby. But these things don't matter at all, because once you are Real you can't be ugly, except to people who don't understand.

I'd like you to meet some women who have embraced this love that has slowly made them real—honest and open and trusting through some of life's difficult passages. They are holding tight to the nail-scarred hand of Christ and will never let go.

*As a prisoner for the Lord,
then, I urge you to live a life
worthy of the calling you have
received. Be completely humble
and gentle; be patient, bearing
with one another in love.
Make every effort to keep the
unity of the Spirit through the
bond of peace.*
Ephesians 4:1-3

When the Applause Stops

Rebecca Stein Morgan

Worship Leader and
Former Attorney
Asheville, North Carolina

Our drama class seemed to be teetering on the edge. The improvisation wasn't working and the usually energetic eleven- to fourteen-year-olds stood listlessly about the room. I looked at Angie. She was groping for a way to redeem the exercise. It occurred to me that a theater warm-up from a recent workshop could save the situation.

"I know what might work . . . ," I began brightly, conscious of youthful eyes turning toward me. But then I stopped.

With a terse and forbidding shake of the head, Angie announced, "Here's what we are going to do."

I withdrew, angry, rejected, and embarrassed. I couldn't physically leave the room, but for the rest of the morning I might just as well have gone home.

It had been a long three days. Angie had arrived Sunday night from Maryland to help with the church's week-long Fine Arts Camp. The theme this year was "The Unity of the Body of Christ." Even though I'm usually pretty easygoing, I had some misgivings about coteaching this drama class. Frankly, I had gotten used to being director of the children's drama ministry at church.

Lots of time was invested in agonizing over scripts, casting, rehearsals, costumes, sets, and especially the performance. How would they be received by this codirector? More importantly, how would I be received? In short, there were lots of opportunities to see how much I need a Savior. He had required me to take some long, painful looks at the idolatry in my life—like living for the limelight, the applause, and hating to share any of it. He had shown me how I crave being indispensable and irreplaceable on stage and off.

Ugh. It is a revolting process—acknowledging what really motivates much of what I do. The strange thing is that I am becoming much more certain, in these lowest of places, that God really loves me. Strangely, too, he has continued to send me, forgiven, right back into those very places where I have been tempted and failed before.

So here I was, with two days of Fine Arts Camp left, unable to face Angie, let alone give up the limelight graciously. But I had met my match in Angie. By the end of Wednesday's class, feeling humiliated and hamstrung, all I wanted to do was to gather up my own kids as quickly as possible and disappear.

"Mom!" Eliza and Rachel raced up to me, eyes shining, and began dragging me back toward the sanctuary. "Mom, there's a recital now for any kids who want to perform something! Let's stay!" I looked down at Sam, who had clearly had just about all the fine arts a normal six-year-old boy could stand, and quickly told the girls they could stay; Sam and I would pick them up when it was over.

In the parking lot, the tears began to roll down my cheeks. Sam, getting in beside me, looked up in astonishment. "What's wrong, Mom?"

I hesitated. "Well, you know how sometimes a friend hurts your feelings?" He nodded. We were both quiet a minute. I began to get an awful, new feeling on top of the hurt ones.

"Sam?"

"Yeah?"

There was that terrible prodding again. Like a heavy hand, firmly prodding, urging me to ask this little boy what I already knew.

"Sam, you know how we've talked about what you should do when a friend hurts your feelings? Do you think I ought to talk to my friend about this, or do I need to forgive her and then try to forget about it?"

The answer I dreaded: "I think you need to talk to her, Mom."

Of all the potential themes for a Fine Arts Camp, why must it be so glaringly impossible to ignore—Ephesians 4 on the unity of the body of Christ? And I'm such a chicken. . . .

"O.K. buddy. Wait for me here a minute." Swallowing hard, I opened the car door wondering whether Angie was still there and what I would say if I found her. I stopped short to see her driving past, alone in her car.

"Angie, Angie, wait!" I got in beside her. "Can we talk?" Somehow the story began to spill out—the series of petty grievances that hurt my pride even to acknowledge before her, but that had built themselves into a hostile wall inside me, shutting her out.

I cried. We cried together. And we talked and prayed and cried some more. Slowly, quietly, something began to change between us. The wall began to come down. As it did, I realized that she felt driven by many of the same doubts and fears.

We made it through the final two days, gingerly. In a cautious and gentle kind of partnership, we began to build mutual respect and trust. Even though we're both sinners, there was reconciliation. Together we had visited the cross, and we knew we could return there as often as needed.

It's still very scary and unpleasant to take an honest look at what often motivates me in my relationships. But this gospel of his, with its call to repent and be forgiven, is really beginning to get to me. I'm feeling safer. And I think, maybe, I'm struggling less to build and protect a reputation.

It's also getting easier for me to enjoy what God is doing in the lives of others as long as I remember that we are secure children of God together.

Becky Morgan says the best part of being forty-plus is *"that I am inwardly being renewed day by day."* She graduated Phi Beta Kappa with a law degree and currently serves on the board of the Gracias Foundation. Becky enjoys leading worship, choir, drama, and women's ministries, not to mention homeschooling her children, Eliza, Rachael, Samuel, and Christopher. She is married to Chip Morgan, a gastroenterologist.

The Lord will fulfill his
purpose for me; your love,
O Lord, endures forever—
do not abandon the works
of your hands.
Psalm 138:8

Something Out of Nothing

Lorie Wallace Barnes

Preschool Director
Boulder, Colorado

The fog rolled in off the rocky New England coast surrounding the circus tent on the campus of Gordon-Conwell Theological Seminary as we in the graduating class of 1978 listened to the British lilt of James I. Packer. Wrapped in blankets at this cool May baccalaureate service, we sat spellbound by his words of wisdom. Each word produced a breath of steam and we shivered in the almost London-like setting.

Dr. Packer spoke on the conversation between Jesus and Peter after the resurrection in John 21—Peter's insistent question, "But what about him?" and the Lord's reply, "Never mind him," "Feed My sheep," and "Follow Me." The next day Billy Graham gave the commencement address and challenged us to be faithful to our calling in Christ. What a rich and memorable weekend!

When I graduated from seminary, the prospect of spending my life in service to the Lord seemed full of hope, significance, and excitement. I wanted my life to count; I wanted to make a profound difference in the world for Christ. In school, I studied the lives of great heroes of the faith and I wanted to be like them.

I had already served in short-term missions in Alaska, California, and Tennessee with Volunteers in Mission associated with the Presbyterian Church USA. My fiancé and I were open to overseas service, believing that together we would make a difference. Our lives of ministry would be a rich, rewarding, and exciting adventure.

But nearly twenty years later, I now view my life and ministry as quite different from what I had envisioned that graduation weekend. Instead of adventure and glory, God has given me challenges and frustration. My life has been consumed by children with chronic asthma, marriage to a very busy pastor, the demands of a large congregation, and the constant struggle of maintaining a household.

While I have been able to use my gifts and training in small ways, most of my life has been lived in quiet sacrifice and, I must admit, not always with a willing heart. There have been times when I was resentful and angry with God at the lot I had been given. I have felt robbed of both joy and contentment. I have wondered, *Where is that deep, inner peace Christ promised to his followers?*

I have found myself at times longing for moments of joy, for a small experience of wonder when God's light would break through the fog and I could once again gain a glimpse of that hope I experienced in seminary.

I am reminded of a passage just before the one Dr. Packer used as his text at my graduation. In John 20, Jesus speaks of peace. He appeared to his disciples following his resurrection and said, "Peace be with you," and showed them his scarred hands. Then he once again said, "Peace be with you. As the Father has sent me, I am sending you."

And finally, when Thomas doubted the resurrection, Jesus said, "Peace be with you. Put your finger here: see my hands; stop doubting and believe." If Jesus meant what he said to Thomas, why don't I experience his peace?

Women tend to be dissatisfied with themselves physically—either our nose is too big or we're too fat, etc. But as Christian women we tend to be unhappy with our spiritual bearings as well. Part of my lack of Christ's peace stemmed from my midlife struggle with life itself.

I was looking for more fulfillment in life than what I had previously experienced. The hard labor of sustaining relationships, negotiating a church community, struggling to find meaning in the ordinary and mundane, and keeping up with being a mother of three boys and the wife of a busy man had left me wanting more. Because I have not been the woman of God I hoped to be, or the mother and wife I longed to be, disillusionment and disappointment have been my constant companions all too often.

Nonetheless, God is showing me that nothing I have been given (including my husband, family, or friends) and nothing I can attempt to do in his name, will ever satisfy the aching in my heart. Those of us who have high expectations of life, ourselves, and God; those of us whose own woundedness and scars seem to be opened time and time again, often find ourselves empty. *And that is God's gift to me.* Now I see that I must empty my life, or have it emptied for me, in order to allow the vacuum of my longings to become something out of nothing.

Who can make something out of nothing? My God can. God made humanity from dust of the earth. He made something from a boy's barely-nothing lunch. He made wine from water—almost nothing. Should I, therefore, be surprised to learn that sometimes God wants to bring us to nothing in order to make something of us?

I have grown to see that *nothing* will give me the peace and contentment I long for until I abandon all I ever want to do and be. Until I come to acknowledge my own emptiness, my spirit will not be released to become that something and someone God wants me to be.

My seven-year-old philosopher recently said to me with a perplexed look on his face, "I don't understand life!"

I responded glibly, "I don't understand it either, David." But there was more to say to my little boy: that God *does* understand my life and knows why I am here; that he often reveals his purposes when we are drained of our desires until it hurts. It is then that we can see that our own lack of contentment and feelings of emptiness are actually God's gift. And if I receive that gift in God's wrapping paper and packaged in his best way—even though it wasn't the gift I wanted—God will make something out of the nothing of my life.

My problem is that often I am like Peter in John 21 who asked Jesus, "What about him?" referring to John, the disciple whom Jesus loved. Peter was concerned about the strong and hard words the Lord had spoken to him regarding the end of his own life, and so asked, "What about John? How will it end for him? What tough row to hoe will you give him?"

I am tempted to ask the same questions of Christ at times when I see the lot in life God has given me. "What about those other brothers and sisters? Can I exchange my gift for someone else's? Is it past the trading deadline? What about him? What about her?" I can only accept God's gift of nothingness when I understand that it was for his glory that I was created and redeemed—that he *can* do something with nothing. After all, the tomb of Jesus appeared to be full of nothing. But there was something going on in God's design. There is more than meets the eye.

I gave Jesus my heart many years ago and I know that he can fill my emptiness. Not because I went to seminary, not because I served him on the mission field, not because I became a pastor's wife, or even because people sometimes outwardly see his peace and presence in my life. Christ can fill the emptiness of my life because long ago I asked him to dwell in the empty tomb of my heart and soul, *and he came in!* He is the author of nothing and he is the author of everything, and by his grace I live.

And, as I seek to celebrate my faith in the Lord after forty, Jesus' prayer in the Garden of Gethsemane is becoming more and more my prayer, too: "Not my will, but yours be done."

Lorie Barnes says the best part of being forty-plus is that *"some people think I'm younger, and I can hike a mountain with the best of them!"* She has a master's degree in Christian education, directs the Promise Preschool, is a freelance writer for Group Publishing, and speaks often at women's activities. Lorie is mother to Nathan, Jason, and David and the wife of Peter Barnes, minister of First Presbyterian Church of Boulder.

*The only thing that
counts is faith expressing
itself through love.
Galatians 5:6*

Hearing the Music

Patricia Jane Gray

Homemaker and Mother
Warrenton, Virginia

I was always confident I would be a good catch for any man! I am intelligent, capable, a good judge of character and circumstances. I have many good opinions (just ask me) and know the best way to get something done (there is my way and the stupid way). I have a fairly high opinion of myself in spite of subtle feelings of inferiority. I am a morally upright person with high standards and expectations for myself and others.

Pour all those godly ingredients into one cute, always slightly overweight female, pair her up with Kevin Gray, and look out!

Kevin and I were both committed Christians when we met in 1972, and we were married in 1975. He loved me and was convinced before God to marry me. I didn't love him, but I was in love with being loved and I was twenty-five. I married Kevin for the music.

How can I describe the music I saw and felt when I was with Kevin during those days before our marriage? It was an aspect of the Christian walk I knew I lacked. It was attractive and exciting, the presence of God's spirit in him—the music of the gospel. I had the words of the gospel, the forms and the discipline, but not the music. I wanted the music.

After marriage, my true self emerged: demanding, disappointed, full of expectations, imposing, full of advice, self-righteous, unaffectionate, and wise in my own eyes. First the music died. Then friendship died. My agenda for the perfect Christian marriage was replaced by loneliness, confusion, fear, and tension. I was surprised! Wasn't I doing things the right way?

After about twelve years Kevin's love for me died. All that remained was commitment to Christ (Oh, thank God for that!), to keeping promises made on our wedding day, and to five wonderful children.

Each year Kevin and I would have one horrible blow-up that would stand out as the worst of all the others. The 1992 argument threatened to be the end of our marriage. Kevin even told me and the children he would be seeing a divorce lawyer and would start sleeping in another room. He did neither of these things, but we did live together in silence, as if divorced, for the next eight weeks.

I am still too blind to trace for you the course taken by God's long arm of mercy as it moved on our behalf. Knowing the corpse of our marriage had been kicked and stabbed again with that last quarrel, we both had little hope left of finding help or escape from our deep, deep pit. Kevin resigned himself to living with me as peacefully as possible, for the kids' sake. I discovered what life must have been like for Jacob's wife, Leah.

During those miserable, silent eight weeks, I immersed myself in God's Word. Crying out to the Lord daily, I read the Scriptures and prayed with empty hands and a profoundly sad heart. My children saw tears of grief every day. At church they saw tears of joy because I knew that this sinful and troubled woman was clean and forgiven in God's eyes.

Then I heard about a conference devoted to teaching, counseling, and encouraging church leaders and spouses. Prayerfully, I laid plans before God and took one step at a time. Could we attend since we weren't clergy? Could I find in-home care for my ninety-one-year-old grandmother who lives with us? Could I farm out five kids? Could Kevin get time off work? Could we afford it? Would Kevin even want to go?

To my amazement, God opened all the doors!

During the conference I was brought back to the basics of the gospel: that Jesus Christ died on the cross in my place and there is absolutely nothing I did or can do to earn or deserve his forgiveness. By his grace, and not by my merits, I am totally and unconditionally accepted by God. The relationship I broke with him has been restored.

For my part, I had taken credit for the work God had done during the thirty years I had been a Christian. I had hidden trouble at home so I would look good. I had been like a Pharisee rather than repentant and humble before God and my family.

All aspects of the conference were healing for me, but it was during our daily hour of counseling that I was able to talk. I love to talk things out, and boy, did I! Figuring at this point in my marriage I didn't have much more to lose, I cleaned house as best I could. I vomited all the sins I could remember and vented much anger. I did not care anymore who knew my darkest secrets. I was completely undone and laid bare.

As Kevin and I talked, I was astonished to realize that the difficult man I was trying so hard to love all those years was daily being destroyed simply by me being me. Through grievous sobs, I asked Kevin to forgive me. And he did.

I haven't tried to change myself in the ensuing three years. I have had too many years of resolving to change, trying hard, and failing. But, to my joy, I am changing! The Holy Spirit within me is doing it for me this time. I have no other explanation. My kids even see some differences.

My prayers have changed, too. Now I pray the Lord will expose my high places and tear them down. I pray he will reveal my sins so I can repent of them. I am learning to pray constantly because I need him constantly. If my perspective and lifestyle is changing, it is becoming one of repentance. Repentance is one key to change that I highly recommend.

After seventeen years of damage, a relationship does not heal overnight. God's miracle in our marriage is that we are on our way. Any progress God-ward has been accomplished through pain and tears, relinquishing control, and surrender. With enough renewed hope and confidence in his power to heal us, I walk with Jesus one day at a time.

I am learning to stop telling God what I think he should do. I repent a lot. I pray for a changed heart—for eyes that see and ears that hear. I ask him to surprise and astonish me. I try to thank him for everything. I want to be like a little child walking with her Father along a precipice. As long as I hold his hand, I'm safe. As long as I put my feet in his footprints, I'll not offend or hurt those I love most.

Best of all, Kevin is learning to love me again! He has forgiven me so thoroughly, it is as if I never offended him. He is telling me his dreams for the future again. Recently he told a friend, "I think I can say now that we're happy for the first time in seventeen years."

Blessings upon blessings, heaped up, shaken together, pressed down, and overflowing! The Lord is restoring the years the locusts devoured. He keeps his promises even to the most troublesome of his children.

And guess what else? Occasionally, I hear the faintest notes of music. . . .

Pat Gray is delighted that being forty-plus enables her to *"have the confidence in myself to tackle new adventures that I did not have when I was younger."* She is a graduate of the University of Virginia and currently teaches her six children at home: Kara, Thomas, Kristine, Samuel, Burke, and Luke (who was born about a year after the life-changing conference). Pat is married to Kevin Gray, a computer analyst.

You open your hand and
satisfy the desires of every
living thing.
Psalm 145:16

Spiritual Surgery
Jeanne Zornes

Author
Wenatchee, Washington

Here we were, forty-year-old Mom and five-year-old son, marking time in the hospital play room. Clad in regulation duck-print pajamas, Zach plodded from one toy to another, turning, touching, enjoying. And Mom fought tears.

The first-born of one who married at mid-thirty, Zach was my special prize. But he came equipped with a throat which threw out a welcome mat to armies of germs. His besieged tonsils hung in his throat like warty lima beans. The night he snored like an idling jalopy, I knew the time had come.

"Yep, they're pretty bad," said the surgeon as he nodded to his nurse to schedule a tonsillectomy. But fear rode along with me to the hospital a few weeks later. My husband, a teacher, remembered when a favorite student didn't survive this operation. What if that happened to Zach?

And so we waited, mom and son. Dad was at work, baby sister with a friend. The anesthesiologist came and appraised his little patient. Finally, the surgical nurse arrived.

"It's time," she said confidently. But doubts hissed as I gave Zach a hug. I'd known parents whose children underwent extraordinary surgeries, many far more life-threatening than tonsils. But this was *my* son—emphasis on the my.

A simple act became my altar of relinquishment. I placed Zach's tiny hand in the nurse's hand. Then I let him go with her down the hall to surgery—for whatever God would allow.

Letting go. How simple, yet how difficult. The world teaches us to grab all we can and achieve all we can. But when God invades our spirits and ambition, that changes. Instead of demanding that God comply with our agendas, we pray to comply with his. We learn to let go, and let God.

"I have held many things in my hands," declared the great German reformer Martin Luther, "and I have lost them all. But whatever I placed in God's hands, that I still possess."

That truth burned into my life a decade earlier. Always the timid, plan-everything-out person, at thirty I'd mustered the courage to start graduate studies two thousand miles from home. If I failed, I could always move back with Mom and Dad for transition time. I thought I had the future tucked securely in my hands.

But death pried open my fist. Mom died of cancer, then six months later Dad died of a heart attack. I had nothing to grab onto. Except the Lord. When my hands emptied, his overflowed into them. How well Psalm 145:16 draws that picture, "You open your hand and satisfy the desires of every living thing."

"Let go," said God. "Drop that little gimme list. Let me put some things of real value in your hands." He allowed grief to deepen my spirit. Eventually he offered the gifts of marriage and children. And then (I hear God chuckling), he took someone who knocked her nervous knees through Speech 101, and spun her off in a speaking ministry.

But as I turned forty and more, I realized that each of these gifts had a shadow: the temptation to jump back in control. The tendency to post a "No Trespassing" sign to God.

How much I held in common with controllers of biblical infamy. Like Jacob, the "heel grabber" twin who schemed to receive unmerited family honors. Could I accept the family roles God chose for me, or would "if only"s cripple me?

Or Achan, blinded by the gold he tucked under the sand in his tent. Could I trust God even in the lean months when the car's fuel pump died and the washing machine choked its last?

How about David, his integrity drowned in a tidal wave of hormones when Bathsheba bathed? When our personalities clashed, could I still love and encourage my husband as God's special assignment? And on down to Diotrephes, consumed with ego at the expense of ministry. When honors came in God's work, would I gloat in the applause or send it back to heaven?

Over and over, I've had to step back, confess my possessiveness, and empty those hands. Like that day in the hospital play room. As Zach waddled down the tiled hall to surgery, I realized this child wasn't my possession. He was God's treasure, entrusted briefly to my nurture.

"The Lord gave and the Lord has taken away," said Job. "May the name of the Lord be praised" (Job 1:21). No grabbing. Just trusting, hoping, letting go.

A few hours later, I reached through the rails of Zach's hospital bed to squeeze his limp little hand. By the end of the day, his grip was stronger as we walked out to the car to drive home.

Both of us had surgery that day. Mine was spiritual.

Jeanne Zornes says that at forty-plus she has *"a fuller appreciation of life's dynamics and the growth of meeting them with the Lord alongside."* A graduate of Multnomah Bible College and Wheaton Graduate School, she is the author of many articles and several books, including the recent *When I Prayed for Patience . . . God Let Me Have It!* In addition to her speaking ministry, Jeanne has been a church librarian and Bible teacher. She is the mother of Zachary and Inga and is married to Rich Zornes, an elementary physical education specialist.

Jesus said to the woman,
"Your faith has saved you;
go in peace."
Luke 7:50

The Path to Mary's House

Karen Schnorr

University Student Minister and
Bible Teacher
Katowice, Poland

The girl slowly approached the Christian book table where I was sitting with students from Bunker Hill Community College. Quietly she glanced at a booklet. "My friend is praying that I'd meet straight people like you—you know, God-like people," she said.

I smiled and invited her to our meetings. For you see, she also was an answer to *our* prayers.

During the next few weeks, I learned the story behind Mary's spiritless and mournful eyes. Nineteen years old, she was a prostitute, a single mom living in the projects, and addicted to drugs. As we talked I knew that I had read her story before. Certainly she resembled someone whom Jesus had described in the gospels.

One day Mary invited me to her home for dinner. I thanked her but suggested we meet in the cafeteria. "No, Karen, my home!" she reiterated.

I thanked her, but once again suggested we meet in my home since I lived close and it would be easier.

Again she responded, "No, Karen, I want to invite you to my home."

A feeble yes slipped out as I agreed. But immediately deep inside I began to scream out, *"NO, NO, NO, God, I don't want to go!"*

One rainy November evening during rush-hour traffic, I was already thirty minutes late and the slow-down challenged my attitude. Holding wet directions, it seemed that I took every possible wrong turn. What and whom was I fighting?

Quietly Jesus impressed on my mind and heart, "Karen, are you too proud to go to Mary's home? To drive to the projects? To see where and how she lives? To allow her to serve you? To meet her son? Are you afraid to know her world and to love her more deeply with that knowledge?"

"Yes." I started to weep uncontrollably.

It's very comfortable to be in control and to surround ourselves with people who are dependent upon us. We can be protective and hide secret areas that are private. Yes, I was a signpost pointing Mary to Jesus, but was I also willing to receive from her? To allow her to teach me and to discover the truths of the gospel together?

My protective walls began to crumble.

I arrived at Mary's house as her guest, knowing that God had enlarged my heart to receive from her. The threat of our differences had diminished and as we exchanged our life stories, I thanked God for the gift of Mary and the challenge she was to my life.

As we said goodbye, Mary thanked me. "Karen, you are the first straight Christian-type person to come to my home. You don't know what this means to me."

"Mary, I thank you. You don't know how much you taught me tonight. I needed to come to your home more than either of us realize," I responded.

I discovered that the biggest barrier between me and this new challenge was that of pride combined with control and power. In order for God to work in our Christian student fellowship, I needed to recognize and surrender completely to him.

That evening was the beginning of many months of fellowship meetings at Mary's home. Mary became a Christian. We hosted a Bible study for her neighbors. Many were either going to or coming from prison. I house-sat and took care of her son when Mary was in the hospital. We cooked together, shopped together, studied Scripture together, and grew together.

Mary and I became friends.

Mark 2:1-12 describes a paralytic man whose friends carried him to Christ in order to be healed. His friends were determined, tenacious, and persistent. They placed him directly in front of Jesus. This is really the only thing we can do for anyone—to place them in front of Jesus.

The paralytic man's friends saw a person with dead muscles. Jesus saw a paralytic man who needed healing both physically and spiritually. All of us need friends who love us this much, and we need to love someone else this much also. To follow Jesus means getting our hands dirty in someone's life and allowing them to enter our life. There is a price tag of love and it is costly. It involves risk to share someone's suffering. But when love motivates us to bring our friend to the foot of the cross, we are all able to see Jesus face-to-face and our lives are transformed.

Our greatest gift is to enter into someone's pain and to be with them—to love them—to bring them to Christ. This is uncomfortable. This is where we are weak—when we face our own pain. But this is also where we can follow Christ in obedience. May we all have eyes that see beyond the surface and see anew with the eyes of Jesus.

> **Karen Schnorr,** at forty-plus, has *"matured enough to finally know the difference between what I need and what I want; trusting God to meet my needs and learning to let go of my wants."* She is a graduate of Queens College and Gordon-Conwell Theological Seminary. Karen has been involved with student ministry for many years and currently serves in Poland with the International Fellowship of Evangelical Students (IFES).

But he said to me,
"My grace is sufficient
for you, for my power is
made perfect in weakness."
2 Corinthians 12:9

Love in Any Language

Maryann Floyd Richard

Cross-Cultural Counselor and
Bible Teacher
Pokhara, Nepal

After a lifetime of privilege, education, and challenging work which made it somewhat difficult for me to understand the full meaning of the above verse, it has finally come to make sense! I certainly feel weak now. As a cross-cultural worker in Nepal, I long to see his power perfected in my weakness. Weaknesses especially in language skills, in my ability to understand the culture and how it influences the people I relate to, and in knowing how to speak spiritual truths into lives full of physical and spiritual poverty.

I'm a mum of three girls under the age of six, a doctor's wife, and a psychologist by training. Currently I'm involved in a variety of Nepali church women's activities and mission responsibilities. I'm a learner even after five years in Nepal and feel that fact most acutely when counseling with the Nepalese.

Presently I am teaching a female leprosy worker how to do counseling. Yet, at the same time, I am very dependent on her for understanding the words and innuendoes of their language that I still do not grasp after years of language study. Even after six or eight years, I will probably still be dependent on Nepali nationals to aid me in understanding their kinsmen.

I am the teacher—yet I am the learner. What a funny predicament! I feel mentally challenged at times when my tongue doesn't follow my thinking and the words come out in a confused mess. Or sometimes I misunderstand a cultural norm, such as the importance of going to people's homes to give pastoral help, rather than having them come to my home.

When will I ingest all the subtle cultural do's and don'ts that aid my goal in getting to know the Nepalese better and care for them more?

As I watch my fellow Nepalis effortlessly speak and listen to their own countrymen, I realize that my desire is there, but my ability is not yet there. I am dependent on them and dependent on God. Does my attitude show this dependency? Or am I arrogant and unteachable, projecting my own beliefs and opinions on others? How do my co-workers see me? Will they, who have been so dependent on educated people from other countries, honestly tell me? Am I seen as humble and open to their opinions, beliefs, and talents?

I certainly hope so.

I have only recently become aware of my dependency versus my self-sufficiency. In the past, my own talents seemed to cover up a need to depend totally on God. Yet now, while preparing lecture notes on basic listening skills for our Bible school, I am thrown into a panic that I will not be able to finish preparing the material on time, and that it will not be explained simply enough for those who can barely read as well as those who have finished school.

Only weeks ago, I cried out to God for help. I asked him for his grace to help me in my weakness, for his glory, not mine. For him to use me, weak and ignorant as I am, to speak to my brothers and sisters in Christ in a country that is not my own. I was amazed at how quickly God seemed to give me an outline of what to say and how to make it pictorially easy to describe. I was increasingly filled with peace and even slept better at night sensing that my work was now manageable and he was there with me.

The beginning lectures and practical exercises went well and I was pleased at the work I had done. But on the fourth day, a subtle dullness or boredom crept in. I had slipped back into doing this all on my own, rather than with God. "Help me, Father, to be continually dependent on you. May I know my weaknesses, even though I outwardly appear strong. May I always claim your power and your enabling. Amen."

Maryann Richard will soon discover the joys of being forty-plus. She is a graduate of Stanford University and holds a master's degree in counseling psychology. Currently she serves on the candidate screening board for International Nepal Fellowship. Maryann is the mother of Jocelyn, Alyssa, and Kirsten and is married to Bruce Richard, a reconstructive plastic surgeon.

I the Lord do not change.
Malachi 3:6

Embracing Change
Dianne Elizabeth Reynolds

Director of Children's Ministry
Washington, D.C.

"I can't wait to go home!" I sigh after an unusually stressful Sunday morning at church. But when I open my apartment door, the silence is not the welcome relief I expected. I go straight to the message pad that my roommate and I keep together.

"Hi, Di, I'm bike riding with Tom, then we're having dinner together with an old friend of his . . . home around ten tonight. Love, Maria."

The words sting, and my disappointment at not having my old companion around to jointly debrief the morning, eat a quick lunch with, or maybe watch a little of the Redskin football game together suddenly is overwhelming and I cry out to God, *"I'm tired of coming home to an empty apartment! I miss having Maria around . . . I hate this change!"*

For five and a half years, ours had been the easiest and most wonderful roommate relationship I'd ever had, and was a great gift in both of our lives. But her growing relationship with a wonderful man resulted in a change in the amount of time we spent together. Though I was excited for her and Tom, and for the many ways I saw God using them in each other's lives, I felt a new sense of lone-liness and I resented God's not filling the void in my life. Through late-night discussions, tears, and prayer together, I came to understand, accept, and support Maria's need and desire to be with Tom. But I still struggled with not having my good friend around at home to just hang out with, as we had done so easily in the past. How I longed for the way it was.

At the same time, there were significant changes taking place at my church, where I work as a director of children's ministry. My great secretary resigned to go back to school; my boss moved to a new position in California, and the youth minister and his wife moved to Colorado for further schooling.

One day, I realized that of the five staff in my depart-ment, I was the only one who had been there more than three months! With further personnel changes, by fall I was the member on staff with the most seniority—after just five and a half years! We laughed about it, but I grew tired of saying good-bye to coworkers and welcoming and training the many new staff members.

In addition, typical for the Washington D.C. area, about eight families moved during the year, and I grieved the loss of those relationships, particularly with the children, whom I'd watched grow both physically and spiritually. Then, to top it all off, after several years of ups and downs, I finally broke off a relationship with a very dear man.

Through all these changes, God has brought me to a new level of communicating honestly with him, and he has been faithful to reveal himself and his truth. I realize that in the past, I had been the great advocate of change, even telling others how exciting it is! But that was because *I* had been the initiator of those changes, such as moving every three years!

The changes happening now were those over which I had no control, and I began to feel that my little world was crumbling—a world I had put a lot of energy into, in order to feel safe, secure and valued. Without realizing it, the Lord was no longer my sufficiency, but rather my created world was my sinful attempt to live apart from God. Frequently the good gifts he gave (such as my work and relationships) became idols, as they were my source of life, security, and identity.

Just recently, Tom and Maria helped me to see that one of my idols is consistency. I want life to stay the same, so I know how to function, how to get my needs met apart from Christ, and bottom line, where Dianne is in control. Out of his love, God has allowed many of these changes in this past year to show me the depths of my sinfulness in depending on myself, rather than Christ.

It's been a hard year; it still is a hard year. I kept waiting for all this to work out before writing this chapter. I wanted to have arrived. But today's deadline reminds me that real life doesn't always end happily ever after. Slowly, painfully, God is allowing me to come to new dependence on him alone, and in that there is great joy.

On one of my darkest days last winter, our senior pastor made a statement during a staff meeting that continues to encourage me: "God loves us enough to keep allowing change in our lives, so that we rely on nothing but him." My prayer is that he will continue to bring the changes into my life that will break me of my need for control, deepening my dependence upon the all-sufficiency of my Savior, Jesus Christ, whom I so desperately need.

Dianne Reynolds is glad to be forty-plus with *"the wisdom God gives through the years—especially* *becoming less attached to needing approval from other people. Instead, I just want to please him!"* As a graduate of Chico State University and Gordon-Conwell Theological Seminary, she speaks often to groups about youth and children's ministry. Dianne is on staff at National Presbyterian Church as director of children's ministry and also serves on the board of Presbyterians for Renewal.

*Unless the Lord builds
the house, its builders
labor in vain.
Psalm 127:1*

The Front Porch
Meritt Lohr Sawyer

Executive Director of a Seminary
Training Foundation
Menlo Park, California

One by one, massive pillars were being lifted into place. I knew all of the dimensions of this front porch by heart. The frame of the roof would rest on each of these nine-foot studs and gently climb to a resting point of twelve feet where it would connect with the frame of the house wall. The width of the porch would be eight feet. It had to be. There had to be enough room for rocking chairs and a porch swing. There had to be enough room for people to be together.

Steve and I were in the midst of an extensive remodeling of our previously purchased fix-it-upper. For months we had been working with architects, determining the best floor plan and design details that would somehow transform this house into a midwestern farmhouse, albeit in California. The front porch had come to represent something much bigger than itself—something to which I had become emotionally attached.

I continued to watch as the porch was being framed by the carpenters. Only months earlier, our architects had come to my front door. How eager I was to start the remodeling at that time. We were already packing boxes and preparing for final bids from contractors. Our architects knew the details of our budget for the project and had been taking it seriously throughout the design process.

The architects didn't know quite how to tell me, but balance sheets have a way of revealing what I didn't want to admit. We could not afford the front porch, they said. It will still be a beautiful home without the porch, they suggested. Of course it would, but I found the tears spilling over before I could even whisper a good-bye and close the door.

Why was this front porch so important to me? As quickly as I tried to tell myself it was only a house, another wave of emotion would signal that I perceived it as much more.

A front porch is a place of rest, of relationships and conversation. It is a place to just be, not a place where one must strive to be what others expect. It is a dream for me to have a place where I am free from striving to overcome my feelings of unworthiness. For years, I have been moving with my hair on fire trying to prove myself. My self-esteem has ridden on the crest of a wave as volatile as a small boat in a storm. I am regularly driven to do something to help myself feel worthy to Jesus, to others, and to myself.

In a quest to prove my worthiness, I started to load up my schedule with all of the right Christian activities. I studied the Bible daily. Steve and I were on the steering committee for our Sunday morning fellowship group. We became deacons. I sat on multiple church committees and took seminary classes. Every social injustice was a new passion for my involvement. At every turn there was a new crusade for Christ. Before our first child was born, four out of five weekday nights we were involved in some Christian work.

With the birth of my first child, I left a computer company and became the executive director of a missions organization. I wanted to be home with my son, so the board agreed to moving the foundation office to my home. Devoting half-time hours to this organization at home allowed more flexibility with my schedule. But boundaries were blurred between my professional and home life. I started to receive business calls at any hour of the day from any part of the world. But no matter, I could always nurse the baby or fold the socks while talking to someone in India.

Because I had the ability to do a hundred things at once, or at least believed I did, I was continually adding more responsibilities to my plate. The kids got older. I just heaped on their activities as well. I could be a mother, active in my kid's classes, and managing a taxi service from soccer to piano to the allergist. I was the president of our PTA.

My Bible study was moved to 6:30 A.M., allowing me to return home just as Steve needed to leave for work. I could always carve out a new time slot. Steve and I would schedule monthly dates with each of the kids and weekly dates with each other. We could fit it all in!

When you're on such a tight schedule, you panic when any part of it has to be adjusted for an interruption. I certainly couldn't be bothered by any piddly issues. I needed to keep moving to keep about the important business of my life—the work of Jesus, important decisions being made about our school system, or whatever pressing item I was on my way to.

I got impatient when a telephone conversation started to ramble. Then there was the time when the automatic dial didn't work, and I resented having to dial the whole phone number myself. I even had to take the time to look up some of the numbers because I couldn't remember them. More work could be squeezed into a shorter period of time through the increased use of those great time savers: computers, fax machines, and pizza delivery.

My life and my Christian faith had become one big project. Much like my house, it was a project to be broken into tasks. Each day I found myself proving my worthiness to God by my ability to accomplish an inordinate number of tasks. In the name of Jesus, I was going to be an incredible Christian! This addiction to a task-driven lifestyle only created a greater need to further load my schedule and challenge my ability to keep more and more plates in the air. Maybe I could impress others that I was worthy.

But I was moving too fast. Perhaps my intentions were good, but my task-driven self was slowly but surely taking over. My head was swimming with tasks. The faces of people I met blurred before me. I was too busy to see the person. Lost was any graciousness. Lost was my ability to share in the lives of others. I was moving too fast to absorb what a friend might have said, much less be able to respond. In the name of feeling worthy to the people I love most, I had instead run the risk of sacrificing those very relationships which are so vital to me.

While *I* have been remodeling a house, God has been remodeling *me*. At age forty, it is time to balance my life of Christian service. I am saying no and relinquishing responsibilities. After spending so many years of trying to earn my worth, I have finally come to realize I never had to. *I am already worthy in Jesus' eyes.*

In trying to do so much and moving so fast, I have damaged the very relationships I sought to nurture and deepen. My front porch is symbolic to me. It is a place where I plan to spend the next forty years of my life—reclaiming and deepening those relationships so dear to me.

In my relationship with Jesus Christ and in those friendships he blesses me with, there I will feel worthy.

Meritt Sawyer believes that at forty-plus we begin to *"feel more secure in the unique person God created us to be."* Her degree in education and master's in education administration have helped her in her current position as executive director of the Foundation for Advanced Christian Training (FACT), which provides seminary education to those from developing countries. Meritt is the mother of Ryan, Kendra, and Clary and is married to Stephen Sawyer, an insurance broker.

Praise the Lord, . . . who
forgives all your sins and
heals all your diseases, who
redeems your life from the pit
and crowns you with love and
compassion, who satisfies your
desires with good things so
that your youth is renewed
like the eagle's. . . . For as
high as the heavens are above
the earth, so great is his love
for those who fear him.
Psalm 103:3-5, 11

When God's Yoke Pinches
Jennifer Hamlett Herrick

Graphics Designer and Photographer
Thornton, Colorado

"I suppose in the past I would have called it faith," Eliza wrote.

I put the letter down and paused to let those words sink in. The reality of faith in God was nothing more to her now than an outgrown childish concept. A series of abandonments had left her peppered with holes like a tin roof that can no longer withstand a light shower. And I guess her faith just leaked out, vaporizing gradually with each disappointment, until there was no substance left.

Now she's pursuing alternatives. Each new Chinese therapy or healing guru offers more than the last. Through sporadic correspondence I have learned how far my friend has walked away from God.

What keeps my own faith from leaking out, I wonder? Why don't I forsake God when his ways are not easy and prayers go unanswered? Why stick it out when hurtful situations don't seem to change, and the people causing the hurt are other dear members of the body of Christ at church or work? Isn't my life slipping by while I wait on God . . . and wait . . . and wait?

There are certain things about being yoked to God that don't make sense on the surface. Yet faith requires trusting the One we're connected to. If I won't be yoked to him, I will, by default, be yoked to another. I choose to constantly come back and check my yoke. Is it really to him or am I temporarily satisfied with a substitute? Even good things can pull me away from him.

When disappointment wraps its blinding film around me and hope is blighted, or when the pain of loss is greater than I can bear, what soft pillow will my tired heart reach out to? Will I turn my back on God for the convenience of my feelings? I hope not.

Sometimes I am scared, too, afraid of being separated from God. I fear not having him near to turn to for help. I am a major struggler. It seems I have to fight for every gain for the kingdom or in my own personal spiritual growth. Beginning with my conversion at age eighteen, my life with God has not been met with joy from my family, but with resistance. Even my Christian husband hasn't always supported my quest for God.

In our married life, we've moved several times to work with different Christian organizations and have seen our jobs phased out with new administrations or budget cuts.

At this time, we're still in limbo as to our future direction. Lack of career stability or success, along with the lack of finances, have been major stressors on our family.

We haven't always had a church situation where we could freely plug in and use our gifts in local ministry. In short, we're a bit misunderstood as intellectual, artsy types. I do enjoy art, music and books, but I love people and long to find a place where I fit for life and ministry. There are times when I feel like I'm on the verge of being swept downstream and I pray the Lord won't let go of my hand. He doesn't. And, in his mercy, time after time he brings renewal.

For example, this year a group of women met weekly to pray for my health. I'm still not free of asthma and allergies, but I have experienced God's love in a much deeper way. I have an increased passion for Jesus and some new close friends in the process. He is filling the holes to keep my faith from evaporating and he's sealing the cracks so I'll be a more useful vessel as he continues to pour his life in me. Even when it hurts, I want to stay yoked to Christ.

Jenny Herrick rejoices that at forty-plus, *"I don't care nearly as much as I used to what people think of me."* She holds an art degree from the University of Georgia and is currently involved in Heartstream—a ministry of restoration and healing for burnt-out missionaries. This self-proclaimed starving artist is the mother of Jeffrey, Nicholas, and Benjamin and the wife of Tom Herrick, an artist currently working as an electrician.

It is for freedom that
Christ has set us free.
Stand firm, then, and do not
let yourselves be burdened
again by a yoke of slavery.
Galatians 5:1

Free at Last!
Sarah Wetzel

Bible Teacher and Missionary
Cochabamba, Bolivia

It was going on 3 A.M. I had been happily looking forward
to the return of my husband after his two-week trip. But
now, even though he was home and lying next to me, I
could not sleep.

It had been a good two weeks. I had enjoyed hibernat-
ing—sewing, reading, being alone, letting my soul catch
up after managing the summer schedules of our four
daughters. I had known satisfying fellowship with God.
So what was this turmoil inside, stealing my peace and
my sleep?

The more details Jake had shared about his trip that
evening, the more agitated I had become. Forgotten were
my good two weeks. *He had a great time, but I missed out,*
I thought. *He met all those interesting people and enjoyed two
new countries!* My thoughts became more weird and dis-
torted. *This trip separated us. We are married and should
refuse to have separate experiences. We need to guard our love.
We should always be together. Then I wouldn't be so hurt by
him now.*

In our twenty years of marriage (ten of them as missionaries), Jake and I have had many times apart. *This difficulty has happened before,* I comforted myself. *I mustn't worry. It's only normal and it will pass in a day or two. Hadn't I read something about roles and relinquishing control as part of the readjustment process after a separation? This is to be expected. Just be patient,* I told myself.

But in the morning my crazy thinking mushroomed. *He'd rather travel, since he had such a good time without me. He likes the other people better than us. He must not love me. Even though he wrote me that beautiful letter, he didn't miss me.* Sick thoughts.

Reading in a book that day about a woman who had problems with her husband's secretary, I saw myself—*jealous!* I was jealous of my husband's experiences, of his life, of the people with whom he spent his time. I was greedy and possessive of his time, ungrateful and immature, suspicious and condemning. I was about as unloving as I could be.

It's normal, I told myself again. But this time the Holy Spirit allowed me no comfort. *I'll do better, just give me time,* I fought back. But I knew what the Holy Spirit wanted.

Down on my knees, I confessed the horrible jealousy. By faith, I accepted God's forgiveness and his peace replaced the agitation. Later, I confessed these sins to my husband and the wall between us collapsed. We were united again by God's forgiveness and his life in us. I could once again believe Jake's love letter.

Solving problems this way is new to me. Before, I believed that our marital problems could be solved by good communication, by being patient (forgiving and accepting), and by following the appropriate how-tos. So I worked at communication, patience, and discipline. Outwardly I was doing most things right and had what looked like a successful marriage and family.

But inwardly I was floundering. The year I turned forty, God used a serious moral failure (near adultery) and months of depression and agnosticism to wake me up to my deep self-righteous hypocrisy. Through an unusual course on Galatians (that showed me how I lived like an orphan rather than a child of God), I gained new perspective about sin, the gospel, God's love, repentance, grace, and how to live in freedom.

Now I know what to do with my sins—take them to Jesus! Simple, yet not easy. It takes the work of the mighty Holy Spirit to break through my pride so that I can even admit my sin. It's much easier to see sin in others! I never see my sin while I'm excusing my thoughts and attitudes as normal, or if I'm thinking that with time or by trying harder I can change.

What *freedom* there is when I stop trying, and simply recognize my sin, repent of it, and let God change me. How many times had my husband returned from a trip to a moody wife who needed time and space to adjust? Now, by God's work of grace, Jake can return to the same (but new) wife who confesses her sin, and is therefore free to welcome and serve him. This is the good news of the gospel for me every day!

Sarah Wetzel says the best part of being forty-plus is *"I no longer have to dread turning forty!"* She is a graduate of Wheaton College and has served many Christian camps in various staff capacities. Sarah is a Bible teacher and mother to Johannah, Miah, Gabrielle, and Caris. She is married to Jake Wetzel, SIM International camp director for Camp Candelaria in Bolivia.

II. WEATHERING STORMS

I know that some people (including my husband and teen-agers) think that Christian bumper stickers are pretty tacky. I can appreciate that; after all, I grew up Presbyterian. But since I'm now over forty and therefore secure, their opinion about this particular subject doesn't bother me.

I put a bumper sticker on our family van. I put it on because the message is so appropriate for this time in my life: "Jesus is my anchor in the storm!"

I don't know about your life, but plenty of storms have been circling around mine for quite a while now. Blame it on the ozone or the government, but let's face it, the weather these days is quite unpredictable!

When I was a little girl growing up in Georgia, we regularly had tornado drills at elementary school. When I lived as a single adult in a California town located right on the San Andreas fault, we were concerned about earthquakes and even had an elaborate emergency plan in our church, should a quake occur during one of the services.

Everyone wants to be prepared for unexpected disasters. But all too often something hits us broadside and we never see it coming. How do you prepare for the potential storms of life—divorce, abuse, infertility, depression, widowhood, cancer? By making sure you are anchored to something or Someone that is rock solid.

In his book *The Life God Blesses*, Gordon MacDonald says that the redeeming virtue of storms is "they force open the doors of the soul, [and] show what's there."

Or as another pastor once challenged me, "When life squeezes you, what comes out?"

Earlier in the same book, MacDonald recalls a conversation with a forty-two-year-old man (my age!) who grew up believing life would be lived without pain, struggle, and inconvenience:

> You have to understand that my generation entered adulthood with the assumption that we would all have good jobs that paid more each year, career tracks that had no limits, marriages that would never grow dull or troublesome, and bodies that would never fail us. I'm forty-two now. I've got friends who've been laid off of work, friends whose marriages are just plain awful, and friends who are having ulcers and heart attacks. A lot of us just don't know how to face all of this. We're just downright depressed.

Sound familiar?

Storms happen to everyone—we will experience them. Sometimes we just have to mature a bit before we realize that we're not the only ones who have ever faced such things. Before I became the mother of a handicapped child,

I was only vaguely aware of a few others in that position. Now I can hardly think of one family who doesn't have at least one child with special challenges of some kind.

When I hit a dark period in my life, which was diagnosed as depression, I felt pretty isolated. That is, until I met and read about dozens of other committed Christians who had also walked that path. I guess one thing that happens at midlife is that we are not quite as shocked when the storms hit. We have lived enough to come to expect them.

But expecting storms and living through them are not the same! What will keep us from being "tossed back and forth by the waves, and blown here and there by every wind" (Eph. 4:14)? The verse just before that gives the answer: Becoming more like Christ. Trusting him. Living in joy, regardless of circumstances. Making a deliberate choice for hope instead of despair. Perseverance, obedience, and faithfulness are not words that slide easily off the tongue, but they are the stuff of which anchors are made.

I'd like you to meet some women who are not just fair-weather believers, but who have hung in there over the long haul. The storms in their lives may be different from yours, but the God they cling to is the same yesterday, today, and forever. During the fiercest of attacks, they were at times driven to their knees and almost washed overboard. But they survived. They dug deep to remember Bible promises and the examples of faithful saints. When life squeezed, what came out was *grace*.

Jesus is my anchor in the storm.

*And I have promised to bring
you up out of your misery in
Egypt into the land of the
Canaanites, Hittites, Amorites,
Perizzites, Hivites and
Jebusites—a land flowing
with milk and honey.*
Exodus 3:17

Prime Time in the Promised Land
Anne F. Grizzle

Family Therapist and Author
Houston, Texas

In January 1989, at age thirty-five, I was facing a move from the Big Apple—where "if you can make it there, you can make it anywhere"—to Houston, Texas, the American boomtown in the sunbelt. I felt grateful to have been able to continue in my career and even publish a book, while still raising my two young children. It was with amazing dexterity that I juggled the balls of a family therapy practice, writing, marriage, and mothering.

Mothering had prevented me from moving full steam ahead with my career. With my youngest now four years old and a new move coming, I felt that I was finally prepared for a grander mission and calling in Houston. With my ten-city book tour still fresh on my mind and an agent ready for my next proposal, I had dreams of a new book. Or perhaps a completely new counseling mission project. Or perhaps an expanded outreach to internationals.

My faith had been alive and well for fifteen years with the usual dips and turns, and my early morning prayers were finally carved out as a well-established routine. As I prayed for vision, I received no clear call but a definite faith work that God was preparing a "promised land" for me in Houston—the details of which would be made clear in time as I trusted him.

In June 1989, the four members of our family piled into our station wagon for our adventurous ride from New York City to Houston, by way of grandparents in Virginia and Atlanta. We were welcomed in Houston by a fierce hurricane. Walking into our newly purchased, beautiful historic home (which the engineer assured us needed only small renovations), we were greeted by hoards of fleas, fifty years' worth of layered dirt that had hidden behind every piece of now-removed antique furniture, and the ever-present humid heat that made the city unlivable until the advent of air conditioning (which, of course, our historic home did not have).

While my husband flew back to New York for business, I holed up for a day in a cool hotel room with my two rambunctious boys. It was then I discovered that I was quite unexpectedly pregnant! Although this may sound like only a small speed bump on my otherwise smooth road, a more apt analogy for me was that of one last ball thrown into a juggler's act, which upsets the whole routine and brings everything crashing to the ground. I was out of control, my limits passed, sick, and depressed.

Rather than deftly managing, I was suddenly struggling to keep my head above water. Instead of a promised land, I was experiencing a spiritual desert from the exhaustion that ruined my well-developed prayer routine. And the "Canaanites" of construction crews, the "Hittites" of heat, and the "Perruzites" of pregnancy were overwhelming giants. Having forgotten that the Israelites' journey to the Promised Land was filled with obstacles, I was not happy to discover my own.

I trudged on as best I could. Three years later, when I had nearly slain these first giants of the land of Houston, two more appeared, perhaps the "Hivites" and "Jebusites." My identical twin sister gave birth to her first daughter, only to find in the hospital that she had the battle of her life on her hands when breast cancer was diagnosed in the course of a postpartum exam.

As I cared for my sister through her various surgeries and mothered her newborn daughter, I was faced with an alarming realization—my own risk of breast cancer was almost one hundred percent! The only prudent therapy was a prophylactic radical mastectomy for myself. I had the surgery, and once again, my plans were dashed against the rock of human limitations and loss. And *this* was supposed to be my prime time of life—the period of "generativity" that Erik Erikson promised to me as the blessings of good psychological and spiritual housekeeping? Most certainly it had come in a form that I had not anticipated. My plans included the same productivity I had enjoyed prior to my arrival in Houston and continued in a linear expanding path after my arrival. Instead, God halted my progress, set me back, and commenced to lay in me a stronger foundation than I had had; a foundation I desperately needed.

When all the balls in my amazing juggling act had dropped, I was given eyes from an observer's view to see it as the game it was—entertaining, challenging, but shallow, a bit absurd, and bound to end. When I was physically cut open and forced to bed, unable to move or do a thing, I experienced an unexpected freedom from doing and from gaining praise from productivity. I lay motionless, observing, dependent; and out of that still spot I had to look, not leap, to appreciate rather than be appreciated, and to hear love from family, friends, and God, not for all I did, but rather just for me.

These deeper lessons of humility and loss had not been my chosen majors in the first thirty-five years of my successful life. Yet, God knows they are prerequisites for any true generativity to come. As my old life of pride and ability is stripped, there begins to show a deeper, truer, freer self of God's creativity. I no longer display my early green leaves of academic degrees and projects accomplished and congratulations for juggling. But I feel my roots growing more deeply than ever, and imagine the fruit that comes will be much richer for my wandering.

I notice now, belatedly, that Scripture notes the greatest offering of the Promised Land is *God dwelling with us—Immanuel* (Exod. 29:46). The milk I see delivered to my door is the sustenance of God's being present in every moment—in my sufferings with strep throat during my first month of pregnancy, in blossoming springtime visits to the zoo, in carefully carved out solitude, and in daily dishwashing.

The honey is in the sweetness of God's appearance in the little lights of life—a four-year-old's amazing "peace be with you, Mom" in the midst of a chaotic day, a flower blooming from the concrete steps to my counseling door, and a friend unsolicitedly delivering to me the very book I'd looked for everywhere. So Andrew, our unexpected third child, and cancer, that robber of body and beauty, have been both wilderness and promised land.

I've also stopped plucking stray gray hairs in my once jet black mane. Not only because gray nearly outnumbers black, but because I am learning to love a Lord of loss who sits beside us in suffering, shines in darkness, and bursts forth from tombs.

I'm grateful God took me in these last five of my forty years by way of desert wandering and giant slaying to reach this unexpected type of promised land. As I peer ahead, I see my prime of life with promises of fruit born of deeper roots, along with multiplying losses. I'm sure I'll need the milk and honey of God's gracious daily presence to walk through both of these from now on.

> **Anne Grizzle** is delighted that forty-plus enables her to *"be on a deeper spiritual pilgrimage and more free to be God's person."* A graduate of Harvard University, she also holds a master's in social work from Columbia University. Anne is a family therapist, leads small groups and Sunday school at her church, and is the author of *Mother Love, Mother Hate.* She is the mother of Benjamin, Joshua, and Andrew and the wife of David Grizzle, vice-president of Continental Airlines.

Fear not, for I have redeemed
you; I have summoned you
by name; you are mine.
When you pass through the
waters, I will be with you;
and when you pass through
the rivers, they will not sweep
over you. When you walk
through the fire, you will not
be burned; the flames will not
set you ablaze. For I am the
Lord your God.
Isaiah 43:1-3

The Furnace
CarolAnn Paul

Director of Conference Services
Winfield, Illinois

The front door slammed and I knew he'd finally gone. I huddled on the floor at the side of the bed, a river of tears flowing down my face.

Everything I had endured in my marriage—my mail and telephone calls monitored, having to walk behind my husband in public, my finances controlled—these and other ordeals were humiliating enough. How could I possibly bear his sexual abuse as well?

When Richard (not his real name) proposed almost a year earlier, friends warned me that they were concerned about the way he treated me. But I wouldn't listen. I convinced myself that marriage to Richard—the product of fourth generation missionaries—was God's will for my life. His seminary training and knowledge of Scripture appeared to me to be the answer to my prayer for help in my own struggling relationship with God.

Now my own pride, overwhelming shame, and the misguided notion that, as a Christian, my life should look perfect, would keep me from revealing to anyone the nightmare I awoke to each new day.

With every new punishment, my stockpile of hatred grew, depleting the insignificant store of love I once felt for my husband. Sinking deeper and deeper into despair, I threw my bitterness and anger at God: "How could you give me a husband like this when all I wanted was a man of God who could teach me about you?" I begged God for the miracle that would bring Richard to his knees at Christ's feet, transforming him into the man of God I had believed him to be when we first met, and fulfilling my dream of a Christ-filled home and marriage.

No transforming miracle occurred. I had done everything in my power to make my marriage work, but my efforts had been in vain, leaving me defeated, depressed, and despondent. Not only did I no longer feel love for my husband, I felt completely drained and empty—as though a great, black hole existed inside me where once joy, laughter, and happiness had been.

I admitted my defeat. I could not love my husband. I could not make my marriage work. I gave up. I had reached the very bottom of myself.

And that was where I discovered God was waiting for me all along.

My stubborn pride and independence had not only precluded my seeking help from family and friends, but had also prevented me from reaching out to God, my best friend. I offered him my feelings of defeat, rejection, and hatred. He lovingly offered his hand and his assurance that I was not a victim of my circumstances, but was sheltered in the embrace of a gracious, merciful, and compassionate God.

As I listened to God's voice through his Word, he showed me not only how much he loved me, but how much he loved Richard as well. Our God is the perfect embodiment of love. He is surrounded by, created of, and immersed in love. His creation of us, Jesus' death for us, and forgiveness of us are all wondrously explained by one simple word—*love*.

As God taught me how much he loved Richard—that for him, he gave up his life, promised never to leave or forsake him, to guide and direct him, to shelter him under his wing and protect him—a tiny seed of love (and later, forgiveness) took root in my heart. Not the selfish love by which I married Richard in order to shortcut developing a Christ-centered life, but a selfless love which enabled me to see Richard for the lost child of God that he was.

Sometimes God delivers us *from* pain; sometimes he chooses to deliver us *through* pain. Daniel 3 tells the story of three men who bore the wrath of the king of Babylon and were thrown alive into a furnace of blazing fire. Like Shadrach, Meshach, and Abednego, I had to experience the fire of the furnace in order to burn off the dross and reveal God beneath the burden of my own stubborn pride and independence.

Though Richard eventually abandoned and divorced me, I realized that God had answered my prayer. The focus of my desire to look more like Christ had shifted to looking *at* Christ.

Our lives are full of situations that threaten to overwhelm us and turn our eyes from the image of Jesus. No matter how hot the furnace you find yourself in, depend not on yourself but on your heavenly Father, who promises to "deliver His servants who put their trust in him" (Dan. 3:28).

CarolAnn Paul says that at forty-plus, *"I'm grateful that I must have the worst years behind me and the best is yet to come!"* She studied at the University of Wisconsin Business College and now directs conferences for Wheaton College. CarolAnn does lay counseling for women in abusive marriages and is a victim advocate for Family Shelter Services of Du-Page County. She formerly served on the international board of Women's Concerns for the World Evangelical Fellowship.

What marvelous love the
Father has extended to us!
Just look at it—we're called
children of God! That's who
we really are.
1 John 3:1, The Message

In Search of My Father

Mary Wilken

Bible Teacher and Writer
Asheville, North Carolina

"Daddy took me out to lunch today!" my friend Liz announced as I ran into her at the dorm. She was beaming and obviously thrilled with the new outfit her father had carefully chosen for her on their shopping trip.

"Terrific," I responded, while feelings of envy and resentment battled inside me. I thought that Liz's experience must be the ultimate ideal for experiencing a father's love. There was a void in my life that never left me and I longed to be in her place.

My father was an alcoholic. Early on he had abandoned any responsibility for our all-female family. My childhood memories are filled with broken promises and endless waiting. Waiting in hot, stuffy cars while he drank with his buddies in bars. Waiting for him to sober up as he lay on the couch. Waiting and hoping that maybe this time he would show up to take our family out together like he promised. So many promises. So much waiting.

When I was twelve my parents finally separated. My father's absence eased the embarrassment I often felt in his presence, especially with friends. I no longer had to make excuses for his behavior. Now that he was gone, I could pretend he didn't exist. Better still, I could create my own fantasy father.

But this arrangement affected me tragically. I tried to appease my hurt by comparing myself to others. It could have been worse—after all, I hadn't been sexually abused or battered. Then a friend gently pointed out to me that abandonment is the ultimate rejection. *Why didn't my father want me? What was wrong with me?* I hated him and myself. Feelings of worthlessness tormented me.

The free love of the 1960s enticed me to look for love in all the wrong places. A long line of boyfriends reinforced the feminist philosophy that the wise thing to do was to use men before they used you. But no one ever explained how to avoid the emotional devastation of this lifestyle. My broken heart threatened to ruin me.

Then I met Terry. Our superficial relationship was typical of college students in the early 1970s. But the Jesus Movement had invaded campuses nationwide and through some friends, Terry became a believer in Christ. His changed life helped me to see the reality of God's love and power. The most amazing thing to me was that Christ loved us even while we were still sinners. He used our less than godly lifestyle to bring me to himself. I surrendered my life to Christ two weeks after Terry's decision.

A short time later we married. Terry's loyalty and love began to prove to me there was a better way—the way to fulfillment was giving of myself, not using others. Seven years later, an older Christian helped me receive forgiveness and healing for my past. "Mary, you know you are accepted in the Beloved now!"

His words overwhelmed my aching heart. But could I believe him? Was I really one of God's loved ones—his child?

In 1985, I had a real breakthrough in intimacy with God. Asked to speak to the women at our church, I was terrified by the situation. The new surroundings intimidated me, as did the giftedness of the people I knew would be there. By determined obedience, I struggled to overcome my fear. I relied on God to help me and give me the words to speak. He reassured me of his presence by giving me peace. It turned out to be a great personal victory as many women later commented on how much it had meant to them. For the first time, I was aware that God was pleased with me. God could be trusted!

A few days later, a couple whom I'd met through my husband's ministry took me to lunch at a favorite restaurant. We had also planned to shop together, and when we arrived at the mall, the woman handed me a one hundred dollar bill saying, "This is for you."

I was dumbfounded. Because I really didn't know them well, the gift seemed to come straight from God. I splurged and bought a dress I had seen earlier. Since it was now on sale, I bought shoes to match. My girlish fantasy had been fulfilled. My perfect Father had bought me a dress!

Shortly after this, my own father called. We rarely had contact, so I was glad to hear from him, until I recognized the familiar effect of alcohol in his voice.

"How are your sisters?" he asked. "You know, Jeannie was always my favorite. Do you think she'd see me sometime?" By this time my older sisters would have nothing to do with him.

He promised to visit me soon. Sure. Calmly, I hung up the phone. But this time, I felt an unusual detachment from his crass rejection. Instead of anger and resentment, I felt a peace that seemed to protect me from everything hurtful he had said. His behavior couldn't affect me anymore.

I believe the freedom I was experiencing came from my *true* Father's love that fulfilled my longing and need. His acceptance enabled me to forgive and love even my insensitive father. Perhaps the missionary Amy Carmichael put it best: "When we come to know our Father of Lights—when we tuck ourselves into God by trusting him as little children—he will carry us through."

Mary Wilken says that the best part of being forty-plus is *"the perspective I've gained through the years."* She works at a Christian bookstore, teaches the "Precepts" Bible study course, and is active in women's ministry at her church. Mary has written many articles and is a contributing author to *The Strength of a Woman*. Mary is the mother of Ryan, Ross, and Jeff, and the wife of Terry Wilken, director of telephone counseling ministries for the Billy Graham Evangelistic Association.

*No eye has seen, no ear has
heard, no mind has conceived
what God has prepared for
those who love him.*
1 Corinthians 2:9

Homecoming Queen Tells All

Linda Jenks

Leasing Manager
Palo Alto, California

I suppose midlife reflection leads most forty-year-olds to the inevitable question: "Is this where I thought I'd be at this point in my life?" Having just reached the end of decade number four myself, that question leads me not only to an immediate response—"not in a million years"—but also to a new appreciation of the understatement in the above verse. I don't know all that God has conceived, but the reality of my life at forty isn't exactly what I had anticipated.

What had *my* mind conceived?

Oh, I'd be living in a house (tudor mansion, actually), full of kids (the attractive, intelligent, always-cheerful variety), married, of course, to a Christian guy (a dark, wavy-haired hunk), with all my annoying childhood issues resolved! We'd camp and ski and sail like I did when I was growing up, and I'd probably be president of Mother's Council at church and the PTA. After all, my mom had been.

Reality? I live alone in a one-bedroom apartment, commute to San Francisco for work every day, and am too exhausted to do much on the weekends. I'm checking out 401K financial plans, and my doctor tells me that my biological clock may have stopped ticking altogether.

Now, that's certainly not *all* bad. After all, "think of the freedom" my friends wistfully comment, as they drive one kid to a soccer game, one to a ballet lesson, and one to karate (they all have to be there at the same time on Saturday morning, of course). And I get to sleep in until 10 A.M., not to mention that I only have six hundred feet of floor space to vacuum.

Nonetheless, it's definitely *not* what I had expected. And I don't say that for the obvious reasons (i.e., the apartment, marital status, no family wagon). No, what I *really* didn't expect was that I would spend almost half of my life in what I call the "food zone"—either struggling with or in denial about the fact that I had a serious eating disorder problem.

Of course, it was my *secret*. As if no one would notice that I'd weigh a whopping one hundred seventy-five pounds one summer and ninety-five pounds the next! Most of the comments I'd get were just polite enough that I could pretend this was nothing unusual. "You have such a pretty face! Wow, if you just lost a few (translation—fifty or so) pounds . . ."

Or the startled, "*How* did you lose so much weight?" which I would of course interpret as either jealousy or admiration of my incredible discipline or my bony arms and legs. Only my closest friends knew how depressed I was most of the time.

Life was supposed to be easy for someone like me. I grew up in a close-knit Christian family, in an affluent neighborhood with a backyard that was perfect for the parties that we had almost every other weekend. I had lots of friends and a great high school and college education. I was homecoming queen and a pompon girl, for heaven's sake!

And, I suppose, I was a classic candidate for eating disorders. High achiever, popular at school, very attached to Mom and Dad, with antennae so finely tuned I could tell when a conflict was brewing two blocks away. The main thing was that I was so *nice* (that word being interchangeable of course with a number of adjectives like upbeat, likeable, friendly, etc.). Yep, a real ornament for Jesus (my therapist came up with that one). I really thought that being a good Christian was all about smiling, being an extrovert, and having it together at all times.

As you might imagine, it was a long process and a myriad of factors that culminated in a moment of grace that changed my life. What comes to mind, however, as especially important in that process were these elements: 1) finally facing truth (i.e., eating lettuce and plain yogurt for months or throwing up after nighttime food binges for weeks on end is not exactly normal behavior); 2) learning, through years of counseling, what it means to be authentic (i.e. telling the *whole* truth, even if it means someone might get mad, or if it means I'm a needy person like everyone else); and 3) undoubtedly the prayers of my parents.

My moment of grace came when I was turning forty and panicked at facing the question "What am I supposed to do now to make my life worthwhile?" All those external cues that I'd been living in response to for so many years just didn't seem relevant anymore. I became aware that the reason this question was always so overwhelming and paralyzing for me was that I was really asking, "What do

I do to make *me* count for something?" And with that came the realization that God's unconditional love for me was something I knew about in my *head*, but didn't believe with my *heart*.

My value has nothing to do with whether I eat plain yogurt every day or if I live on "3-for-2" packs of Twinkies; with how happy my family and friends are at any given moment (assuming of course, that it's my job to make sure how they are); or with just how nice I am and how together I appear.

My equating being a good Christian with needing to have it all together had prevented me from experiencing the truth of my condition—*that I, like everyone else, am weak and am a sinner and in need of God's grace and love.* In fact, God probably expects more failure of us than we do of ourselves. He sent Jesus because we don't have it all together. What incredible freedom to know that there is *nothing* I can do that will cause God to love me any more or any less than he does at this moment! All I have to do is to let him love me and then I can experience abundant living and let him love others in an authentic way, through me.

Everything has changed for me—ironically, in my fortieth year, when everything was supposed to start going downhill. With that glimpse of God's unconditional love and grace came the miracle of freedom from my twenty years of eating disorders. But just as miraculous is the peace that I can now experience in spite of unfulfilled expectations, in spite of my circumstances. I truly would not trade that peace for anything.

Linda Jenks at forty-plus is glad to be *"finally accepting the fact that life and growing are more about* *'downs' than 'ups.'* " She holds both a bachelor's and master's degree from Stanford University and works in San Francisco at Insignia Commercial Group. Linda enjoys discovering biblical truth through Bible Study Fellowship.

"For I know the plans I have for you," declares the Lord; "plans to prosper you and not to harm you, plans to give you hope and a future."
Jeremiah 29:11

Someone Finally Heard Me

Elizabeth Emery

College Chaplain and Dean
Beverly, Massachusetts

The wind picked up to hurricane force as rain pelted our house. Suddenly, there was a loud crash that shook the house and plunged an already dark night into an even deeper darkness. I was awakened by the noise and frantically climbed out of bed. In the darkness, I lost my bearings. There was no light to guide me down the hall to my parents' room. I cried out for my mother and father to come, but no one came. No one heard my cries.

You see, both my parents were deaf and had been so all their lives.

I bumped into beds and chairs and walls trying to find a way out. From the darkness, a chubby little hand reached out for mine. It was my twin sister, Jane. She pulled me toward the door and out into the hall. She had heard my cry. I was rescued by my three-year-old twin sister. She comforted me as she led me to my parents' room.

From that night emerged a theme in our lives—that of crying out and not being heard. So we took care of each other. At times, we also took care of our parents. We would interpret for them when someone called on the phone. When we went shopping, we would explain to them what the salesperson had said. If an ambulance came upon us with siren blaring, we would tell them to move over to the side of the road. They were our parents and we dearly loved them, but at times it felt as if we were losing precious parts of our childhood.

An even deeper darkness than that which I experienced at age three descended on me thirty-three years later. I was divorced by a husband who had fallen in love with a parishioner, sexually abused by a Christian therapist whose task it was to help me heal from that divorce, and had severe episodes of depression that sometimes came out of nowhere. Like the woman who touched the hem of Jesus' garment, I had spent all I had on many doctors and was no better.

Months of darkness turned into years. I felt as if I were losing precious parts of my young adulthood. At times there seemed to be no future, no hope. No one knew how deep the darkness had become. How could I let them into my private hell? After all, I had given the outward appearance of being a successful young woman. I was well educated, articulate, capable, and respected. I had completed two master's degrees and was an ordained clergywoman. Yet I felt as if I had to perform for the world.

One day, the performance came to an end. The pain was too great. I cried out in agony, fearing no one would hear and no one would come to rescue me from this darkness I had become trapped in. But someone did come. In the midst of that darkness, I came to understand that even in the darkest night, there was One who was always present, One who *would* hear my deepest cries.

That day of agony and realization turned into weeks and into months. Each morning I would leave my room and go outside to view the beautiful autumn countryside. I was safe and felt cared for. I opened my Bible and prayed the Psalms. I talked with God. I wrote endless pages in my journal. After eighteen years of what had been a living hell, my depression was finally diagnosed and treated. I discovered that what I had was an illness, not a weakness. God had given me back my life. Healing had begun.

Years have passed. I have struggled with trying to forgive myself and those who hurt me, and with an illness I had no control over. I came to a truer understanding of the meaning of God's forgiveness in my own life. God has shown me again and again that my suffering is redeemable as I place that suffering in his nail-pierced hands. God also has given me gifts and graces beyond imagining. It has made the struggle worth it. For me the adage "Life begins at forty" was literally true!

Today, I sit in my living room with a college student. She cries out in pain. She has been sexually abused. I know her life will never be the same again. She feels as if she has nowhere to turn. I listen. I cannot take away her pain. But I know Someone who can redeem that pain. A long journey is just beginning in her life—a journey that will not always be easy. There will be rough places along the way and places of rest. It's a journey that has a future and is filled with hope.

I look beyond the young woman seated next to me. I am reminded once again of the verses that hang framed on my living room wall, "For I know the plans I have for you," declares the Lord, "plans to prosper you and not to harm you, plans to give you hope and a future" (Jer. 29:11).

Elizabeth Emery says the best part of being forty-plus is *"integrating all of life's experiences from my first forty years."* She has a degree in elementary education and masters degrees in deaf education and pastoral counseling. Elizabeth is the college chaplain and dean at Endicott College and also serves on the board of the Beverly School for the Deaf.

He made him ride on the
heights of the land and fed
him with the fruit of the
fields. He nourished him with
honey from the rock.
Deuteronomy 32:13a

Honey from the Rock

Penny Nickel Hagaman

Historical Interpreter
Black Mountain, North Carolina

I sank to my knees, burdened by the weight of the large aluminum canoe riding on my shoulders. The end of the nine-mile Grand Portage trail on the border between Canada and America was within my grasp. Only two more miles to go if I could just struggle to my feet.

My assistant leader was far ahead of me, carrying our Duluth pack. The group of teenaged girls whom I was leading on this three-week wilderness trip was nine miles behind me. I was alone and in a tough situation. I was exhausted and knew I couldn't muscle the canoe back onto my shoulders if I let it drop off.

As I fought to regain my footing, an overwhelming thought occurred to me: In a minuscule way, my struggle with the canoe was similar to what Jesus must have felt as he shouldered the heavy cross beam on the way to his own crucifixion. He not only suffered under this physical burden, but he also carried the weight and burden of my sin.

Tears filled my eyes as I related more now to the pain he suffered for me. I would never again look nonchalantly at the Cross. I finished that trail with a new love in my heart for my Savior.

Fifteen years later, another burden weighed me down as I awoke in a hospital bed following surgery. I had been diagnosed with breast cancer, and was in recovery from a modified radical mastectomy and major reconstructive surgery. I was unable to move, and surrounded by countless machines and medical paraphernalia.

My thoughts returned to that portage trail, where I had also been "paralyzed," unable to move. My heart slowly ceased its panicked beating as I remembered God's overwhelming love and faithfulness to me. As I listened to praise music and read the Psalms during that week in the hospital, I was filled with joy and the all-encompassing sense of God's love for me.

Psalm 131:2 became my touchstone: "But I have stilled and quieted my soul; like a weaned child with its mother, like a weaned child is my soul within me." A weaned child is able to totally relax in a mother's arms and not be filled with anxiety of rooting around for milk. So it was with me.

Hudson Taylor, the great missionary to China, stated, "It does not matter how great the pressure is, but where it lies; if it comes between you and God, or if it drives you closer to the heart of God." I could not change my situation, but I could change my response to it. I chose to let this hard "rock" of cancer drive me closer to my heavenly Father. I chose to rest near his heart.

Six months later I watched helplessly as Steve, my strong, athletic husband, underwent a wrenching and life-saving bone marrow transplant for leukemia. My mind cried out for healing for us both, but my heart was at rest with God's purposes, even when I didn't know what the future held.

Other families in the hospital questioned whether I was angry at God for allowing us both to have cancer, especially since we have two young children. I'd tell them that I wasn't exactly overjoyed to be a cancer patient, but I wasn't angry with God, either. On the contrary, I was trusting God's unfailing love for me that would be there whether I lived or died. He had never deserted me in the past, nor would he do so now.

I had been a Christian for many years before my confrontation with cancer and all the implications that go along with a life-threatening disease. Through the years I've had wonderful opportunities to grow in my faith. My life was molded by strong Christian parents, a Christian college, and through the Christian colleges and camps where I worked. When the drought hit, my well was full of Jesus' living water.

However, there were times of fear and doubt because occasionally my focus shifted to my circumstances and away from the One who is sovereign over all circumstances. God has truly given me everything I need for living a good life, whether well or ill. But I must appropriate my faith and trust in him. Too often we see things in such a temporal way while God is viewing our lives for eternity.

The seemingly hopeless "rock" of cancer has yielded the sweetest honey in our lives. Even during the darkest hours of our illnesses, God gave us a deep peace—peace that was overpowering in contrast to the chaos of cancer. Every day is a gift from our merciful Lord, and we know that Jesus is real because we have witnessed the miracle of his peace in our hearts and minds, in the midst of an often frightening world. "I call as my heart grows faint: lead me to the Rock that is higher than I" (Ps. 61:2).

Penny Hagaman, at forty-plus, enjoys *"looking back and seeing God's faithfulness, not to mention never having to face adolescence again!"* A graduate of Wheaton College and Mankato State University, she is a retired educator and former camp administrator, and currently works as an historical guide to the Biltmore House in Asheville. Penny has served on the boards of Christian Camping International and the American Red Cross. She is the mother of Jessica and John and is married to Steve Hagaman, manager of the Billy Graham Welcome Center at The Cove.

*And the God of all grace, who
called you to his eternal glory
in Christ, after you have
suffered a little while, will
himself restore you and make
you strong, firm and steadfast.*
1 Peter 5:10

Suffering
As Honor
Janice Berkeley

Writer and Post-Graduate Student
Canada

Several years ago, when the actor George C. Scott failed to show up for his Academy Award, my young mind wondered how anyone could refuse such an honor. I'm learning, though, that human accolades may not be such an honor after all. Mother Teresa, the Albanian nun who works with the poor in Calcutta, views *suffering* as an honor, a privilege, a mark of God's approval.

A few years ago my sister told me that our father had sexually abused her. Every alarm bell in my system began its clangor. I knew instantly and with certainty that she was telling the absolute truth, while also thinking she was totally crazy; also knowing something had also happened to me, and wondering how we could possibly accuse him without any proof.

The one thing I knew without question was that I needed help, and soon. I waited months to see a particular counselor, then more months to get into a weekly spot with her. Why? Because I knew she had suffered. Before I even began my search, I told my husband, "Whoever counsels me will have to have suffered." I knew I would only trust someone who had been through the furnace, whose shell of certainty had been irremediably cracked, who had healed, had overcome bitterness, not to become good as new, but permeable, open to the immense, confusing reality of life.

Further, I needed someone to model how to suffer expertly, or at least deeply and with grace. Some days this is all I hope to be when I grow up—someone who lives out for others how to suffer graciously.

My own suffering has included the usual difficulties and some unusual ones. A small group of disgruntled church members rebelled at the loss of their power and undertook a prolonged personal attack against their pastor, my husband. We lost our home and financial security. My belief that God works justice in his institutions, especially the church, was shattered. Another time a man attempted to abduct our daughter from our church a few years ago, and our church failed to respond at the time in any pastoral way to our trauma. Later, in one freak accident, I lost my ability to run or to undertake a lot of other beloved activities, such as hiking. All this in the past ten years!

The effect? Suffering has softened me. It has cracked my shell of ego and has shrunk my imagined sphere of power and influence. *Despair sometimes opens doors which hope can't budge.* I am more whole, strong, clear. I've participated by his grace in a very small portion of Christ's own suffering. I can recommend it almost without reservation as a strengthener of the soul.

Nonetheless, I must admit that right now I'm on George C. Scott's side. I've had enough honors of this particular type. The next one can go to someone else. Really. I won't mind. This is in part because I have endured a huge amount of another, far deadlier kind of suffering. I have suffered almost unbearable confusion.

When a friend moved, or I lost a job, or even when my half-uncle (a drug dealer my age) was executed by the mob, I may have been confused about why the events happened. But at least I could locate the source of my emotions. My grief, anger, and frustration had reasons.

But in these last few years, I have sometimes experienced emotional confusion so extreme it has dwarfed even the horrifying recognitions which were arising. I slowly grasped that I didn't exactly have repressed memories; I had repressed states so complex they could be described as people, and *they* had the memories. I suppose I have to use the jargon: multiple personality. I hate to do so because the public perception is so governed by dramatic movies and books such as *Sybil*. The reality for me and for many others is that this coping mechanism more often stays hidden than not, and many people never live the split lives of the popular conception.

I now recognize that this splitting off of pieces of an original whole was a brilliant strategy for coping with unbearable pain and degradation. There was literally too much trauma for one child to stand, too much for one consciousness to bear. So sometime in my very early childhood, there began to be more than one child, one consciousness. This process allowed one part of me to survive and grow—incomplete, deeply wounded, but functional.

Nonetheless, I have also asked a set of questions very like those asked of others in my situation: "If all this really happened to me (and I did all the things I remember), how can I go on living? If I am just a psychiatric freak, who will ever want to have anything to do with me? Am I so damaged that I will never be a complete person? Am I so dirty that no one will ever want me? Can I endure all this pain and survive? Is there any way to live a dignified life?"

An answer to some of these questions came one Good Friday. I have never liked the cross at the front of our church. Nonetheless, Christ was suddenly there in my mental eye. Not only guilt, but all the world's shame was flowing to him. Shame so great I had not yet faced it was moving in rivers into that greater heart.

I could see with my inner eye that my own shame, the all-permeating fact of what had been done to the most intimate crevices of body and soul, had been converted by grace into cleanliness. I've known before that not I, but my abusers, should bear the shame. Now I began in fact to feel clean.

Another turning point was the realization that my friends and family recognize me. They see me as real, as a person. Further, I have had a relationship with God. In those two facts, whatever label I give myself, I find responsibility. There are times when I only know that I am who God, or a friend, or my child, sees me to be.

For the first fifteen years of my faith, I accepted the dogma that I had to do myriad daily or weekly things to keep it real. I sought assurance in others' beliefs. Above all, I refused to test that faith, mortally afraid that this thing which had ordered my chaotic life, which had protected the best parts of me, had nourished my starving core, would somehow be proved untrue, unreal. Ha! As if I could somehow by force, thought, or effort keep this faith which originally gave itself freely to me.

In the end, although I nearly suffocated it first, I made a decision about my faith. I opened it up, let it breathe. I had to give up my pre-existing understanding of faith, to accept confusion. I also had to turn inward, to decide for myself, to ask, "What is real *for me*?" In testing the reality, I began to see the false dichotomies: I am somewhat ordered and sane, even though brutally abused. Faith may not fail, but thrive when opened to the world, when tested.

I still have no answer to the theological question of whether faith is more like a fickle cat—prone to wander off if not cosseted, or like a slavish dog—willing to stay no matter how badly mistreated. I do know this: I can stand firmly only on the ground of a tested reality.

I hope to die a believing Christian. On my good days, when I *feel* my belief, I can say without hesitation, "Eternity has grasped me and will not let me go." On the bad days, when I only *know* my belief, when what I feel like is a mere pile of dust, or worse, I can still say, "This one is beyond my control. Whoever, whatever I am, I can't make this thing called faith happen." There is peace in either state.

If my hope is realized, I will still be saying what I say today: I have not kept the faith; I have *been kept in faith*, and that by grace alone.

> **Janice Berkeley** (a pseudonym) says that *"growing sane"* is the best part of her forty-plus life. In addition to her writing and studies, she has a master's degree in science. Janice is the mother of three children and the wife of a chaplain.

Be imitators of God, therefore,
as dearly loved children and
live a life of love, just as
Christ loved us and gave
himself up for us as a fragrant
offering and sacrifice to God.
Ephesians 5:1-2

A Worthy Struggle
Deborah H. DeFord

Author and Curriculum Editor
Storrs, Connecticut

"I'd love to see you!" my friend Emily said over the phone. "I'm not doing anything much, just sitting around being decorative. Give me a call when you get to Maine."

Two weeks later, my family and I drove down the rutted gravel road to a small enclave of summer cottages nesting on the verge of Penobscot Bay.

It has been several years since we last visited Emily here, more than a year since I last saw her. But the converted barn that is her summer place looks the same, familiar and welcoming amidst the splash of wildflowers and the warm scents of salt and pine and mossy earth.

She greets us at the Dutch door and within moments we are deep in conversation and laughter. Emily regales us with stories of mutual friends and quirky happenings, asking us the kinds of questions that show that she has known us for a long time and loves us enough to know what questions to ask.

Hours later, as the afternoon shadows begin their final stretch, we make our farewells. When we drive away, hands waving out of every car window, a piece of my heart remains behind. But with me I take a new stack of stories and wise observations and warm memories through which I will page over the coming weeks and months. It has always been this way with Emily, and the fact that she is eighty-five and in constant, often crippling, pain has not diminished her effect.

I was a young teenager when I first met Emily—in her fifties, wife of the pastor at our suburban Philadelphia church, the principal of a Christian school, co-host to one of the most successful college-and-career ministries I've seen, and a Bible teacher who drew crowds and held students on the edge of their seats for weeks with a single Scripture passage. She was a star in our small world whom I viewed from a distance.

She saw me in far more earth-bound terms. She attended my baptism, a gleaming day of confirmation and commitment. But she also watched me abandon the tenth-grade Sunday school—an uninspiring class on the dos and don'ts of teenage life—for the College and Career discussion group, then in the middle of a lively study of C. S. Lewis's *Screwtape Letters*. When a parent insisted loudly that I be sent back to my own age group, Emily watched me drop out altogether.

She was certainly aware that I went on to exercise inappropriate teenage behavior, because she attended my (emergency) wedding, performed by her husband at the end of my junior year in high school. I didn't realize at that time how unacceptable my behavior had been to many church members, and how unusual and gracious Emily's attitude toward me was. Years later, a former Sunday school teacher came to an evening gathering at our church, and approached me afterwards.

"I want you to forgive me," she said, as she took my hand and her eyes filled with tears.

"Forgive you!" I stammered. "For what?"

"I've thought ugly, unforgiving thoughts about you since your . . . trouble," she said.

In the midst of Emily and Dick's openhearted acceptance, love, and care during that time, my bad reputation became irrelevant to the good work God was doing in me.

Four years after our wedding, I was a correspondence high school grad, the mother of two small daughters, and moving to Connecticut for my husband's graduate education. Coincidentally (and providentially), Emily was moving to the same area of Connecticut. She and her husband, Richard, were starting a new church and they quickly gathered my young family into the heart of their ministry.

When Emily suggested I would be great in Sunday school leadership, I hemmed and hawed. My experience with Sunday school, after all, was less than outstanding, and I knew the stellar company I was keeping in Emily. "I'll help," I grudged. "But I will not teach!" Of course, what I *knew* I could not do (and thought I did not want to do) is exactly what Emily coaxed, taught, and encouraged me to do. I'm doing it still. I can't imagine not teaching when the subject matter is the most important, life-changing material for all eternity.

Emily did a lot more than lead me, by example and training, into a life's ministry. She became my dear friend. When my husband was unemployed over a period of years, she stood by me. When her husband died abruptly and seemingly too soon, I stood by her. We met for prayer and Bible study for a number of years, and Emily acted out the best of what Christian love is all about. She shared who she really is. She suffered openly, counseled wisely, pulled no pious punches, and kept on in her own life and ministry, come what may.

I remember one time, when I was agonizing over what seemed like unanswered prayer, I asked Emily, "When does it get easier?" She threw back her head and laughed with her whole soul.

"Never!" she cried, and then added, *"but what a worthy struggle!"*

Now, with Emily in her eighties and me in my forties, she is still leading the way, still walking alongside me, and rejoicing with me in my recent twenty-fifth wedding anniversary. Before we left her on that beautiful Maine afternoon, she made a comment that has become my latest byword.

"Minister's wives ask me all the time what they need to do to be good as the spouse of a pastor. I say, Be yourself," and with a gleam in her eye she added, "only godly."

Emily has known who I really am for thirty years now. And at one critical point after another, she has accepted the real me, while encouraging and leading me toward godliness. Just as Christ simultaneously leads the way and walks at our sides, Emily took me by the hand and changed the course of my life. It is exactly those qualities that will allow me not only to keep the faith, to look for and follow God's leading, but to take on another generation of God's children and help to lead the way.

Debbie DeFord is glad to be forty-plus and have *"the courage and confidence that grows through years lived in God's loving embrace."* A graduate of Eastern Connecticut State University, she stays busy as a teacher, editor, and speaker. Debbie has also authored several books, including *Sarah Bush and Her Town* and *An Enemy Among Them*. She currently serves as chair of adult education in her 2,800-member church. Debbie is the mother of Kimberly, Gabrielle, and Ethan and is married to Ronald De-Ford, a management consultant.

*He will call upon me, and I
will answer him; I will be
with him in trouble, I will
deliver him and honor him.
Psalm 91:15*

The Crash
Sally Wilson Pereira

Pastor's Wife
Black Mountain, North Carolina

August 29, 1991, was the fourth day of school for my young daughters Mary and Emily. I was glad when they jumped into my car right after the bell rang that afternoon. It was beginning to rain lightly and we had to pick up my husband's new publicity photos at a photography studio across town before heading back to our home.

The girls were happily telling me about their new kindergarten and second-grade teachers, their friends, and what they had done that day, when I had to stop on the four-lane highway because traffic ahead was standing still. I was looking for an opening in the next lane so I could get around when I glanced in the rearview mirror and saw a heavy van flying around the curve behind us.

I had time only to say, "Girls, hang on. We're about to be hit." I can still feel our car being crushed into the car ahead. I can still hear our cries and screams of horror and our station wagon rocking as the driver of the van moved his vehicle back and forth to turn it sideways, trying to make it appear that he had tried to avoid us.

I turned to see if the girls were okay and they began to scream hysterically. I looked in the mirror at my face and saw what had frightened them. Even with a fastened seat belt, my head had hit the steering wheel and then had been thrown back against the door frame. My teeth were knocked loose. My nose was broken. My face was bleeding profusely and beginning to swell.

If my neck had been broken, I would have finished it off, because in my fear for my children, I turned around and tried to help them carefully crawl out of the shattered glass into the front seat. No one stopped to help. I remember screaming, "Oh, God, oh, God, please come and help us!"

After what seemed like a long time, some firemen appeared. I begged them to stop the bleeding. They got some rubber gloves and gave me ice and a cloth to do it myself. Finally a policeman arrived. He was not as gentle as the fireman, and in the midst of a barrage of questions, I said, "Please be quiet for a minute." The girls were calling for their daddy and were crying. I bowed in prayer as I touched them both and asked God to care for us. I reminded them that God was right there in the car with us, and that he loved us then as much as he had that morning when we prayed for safety through the day.

Out of a four-vehicle accident, I was the only person injured. The girls grabbed my purse and glasses and scrambled into the back of the ambulance. We were separated at the hospital and I had to trust God to protect them until Jerry could find us. Our full-sized station wagon was totalled, but we were alive! I will never be pain-free, but my teeth firmed back up and my nose healed. That experience will probably always be a part of us.

The nightmares, the loss of faith in some aspects of law enforcement, the awareness that there are drivers who have no insurance, and the fear of driving and riding in cars have lessened somewhat with the passage of time. But not a day goes by that we do not realize that each day is a gift from God and that life is fragile. His goodness does not depend upon what happens to us. He loves and cares for us on bad days as much as he does on good days.

Every day I read Jeremiah 29:11 on our kitchen plaque and realize how its meaning has deepened for me through the years. "For I know the plans I have for you," declares the Lord, "plans to prosper you and not to harm you, plans to give you hope and a future." I remember when this became my favorite verse.

It was at a time when my girlhood dreams seemed to be coming true. I was planning to marry a young preacher when the unthinkable happened: one month before our wedding we cancelled everything, and he left town. My heart was broken, but my eyes were opened. I thought God had mocked my prayers. He let me kick and scream and loved me through it all. I slowly saw that he had answered my prayers, only not in the way I had planned. The hurt, mistrust, and humiliation were gradually replaced with acceptance, peace, and joy when, eleven years later, God brought into my life the man he had been fashioning to be my husband.

He replaced shallowness with depth, deceit with integrity, counterfeit ministry with the genuine, and infatuation with lasting love. Many times I have shouted "hallelujah" that he made me wait for his time.

God has given us two healthy baby girls even though I was in my late thirties when they were born. But when little Mary was not even two months old, she underwent surgery. Afterwards, the doctor told us she had cancer, probably a rare, aggressive kind. We fell back into our chairs in the waiting room in disbelief.

But God spoke to my heart and I said, "Doctor, we wouldn't even have this baby if God hadn't given her to us two months ago. He loves her more than we do. He made her and he can fix her. We're going to trust him." In our agony we cried wet spots in our carpet. Later a team of medical experts at the Mayo Clinic examined the tissue and assured us that the word *cancer* should never have been used.

Now when I see my little girl balance on two feet (one with a small scar) on the balance beam in gymnastics, I say, "Thank you, Father. You are so good!" Because I can look back and see how he has given me a future and hope in the past, I've learned that I can also look forward in faith, knowing that I can trust God with the rest of my life.

Sally Pereira is relieved to be forty-plus because *"I don't have to worry about turning forty anymore!"* She is a graduate of Wheaton College and teaches Sunday school and Awana clubs. Sally is the mother of Emily and Mary and is married to Jerry Pereira, the minister of the First Baptist Church of Swannanoa.

*May the favor of the Lord our
God rest upon us; establish
the work of our hands for
us—yes, establish the work of
our hands.*
Psalm 90:17

Inventory
Specialist
Jeanne Zornes

Author
Wenatchee, Washington

My friend Peggy hadn't meant to crack a joke.

I'd just gotten a call from my doctor about my annual
mammogram. He ordered a breast biopsy to check suspicious spots. The big C-word—*cancer*—dimmed my future.
My mother had died of cancer at fifty-nine. Would I, now
forty-five, repeat her health profile?

Peggy knew that concern burdened me as we talked
about transportation and meals for my family the day I'd
be out of commission for the biopsy.

"Don't worry about a thing," she said in her usual helpful way. "I'll bring your family dinner after your autopsy."

There was a silence.

"I'm not that bad yet," I replied with a laugh, correcting
her word confusion.

But the possibility that a killer lurked inside my body
seemed to strangle my spirit. I had too much to live for—

not the least being my two young children. I wasn't ready yet to say with Paul, "To live is Christ, to die is gain."

Lab problems delayed results on my biopsy for weeks, forcing me to live hamstrung by uncertainty. I sewed up my stack of fabric. I cleaned out my desk. I purged files. I read my Bible, aching that there was so much I didn't yet know about the God who crafted my body—who understood why cells would go amuck.

Friends offered advice and books. My bedside reading stack ranged from breast reconstruction options to self-cures through eating special grasses. But they didn't get down to the deepest pang, the yearning to know: Who am I? Why am I here?

Then one day a large, flat envelope arrived in the mail. Inside was a parchment of original calligraphy bearing portions of Psalm 90:

Our lives are over in a breath;
Teach us to count how few days we have
  and so gain wisdom of heart.
Let us wake in the morning filled with Your love
  and sing and be happy all our days.

The verse was inked by an unexpected source. Long ago in grade school, I'd been in Camp Fire Girls. Through the years, usually at Christmas, I'd kept in touch with the leader, Mrs. Innes. Her husband, always the silent type who winked at us little girls as he passed by the rec room, had taken up calligraphy in his retirement.

Mr. Innes had chosen that verse and his wife had mailed it to me—just when I needed it. I rearranged the plaques on the wall above my sink and put it right in the center. Washing dishes, peeling potatoes, amidst the mundane of life, it probed my soul.

As I looked beyond the words of the verse to the measured strokes of each letter, I started to get my answer.

God asks us to count our days. But he already knows the sum. After all, he is the inventory specialist. He can corral infinity. He has numbered and named the stars (Ps. 147:4), whose unknown masses stun contemporary astronomers. He has numbered the hairs on my head (Matt. 10:30), even when that number changes with each yank of a brush. And he has bottled my tears (Ps. 56:8), measuring each drop that escapes from an emotional or physical wound.

I added a few extra tears those weeks I waited, avoiding hugs on the sore side of my anatomy. They flowed when I focused on the first part of that psalm, the sober admission that life is very brief. But when I meditated on the other lines, my tears turned to trust.

We count our days so that we may gain wisdom. My tendency is to misread that to mean "we make our days count so that we may gain wisdom." That's typical of someone whose personality bends toward time management and production quotas. And that's not all bad. Time is a treasure prone to robbers, especially those things which would keep us from God's Word.

But the verse says God teaches us to count our small portion of days. Measured against eternity, they're just a blip. Yet each one is important to God. Why? Because each offers a fresh opportunity to awaken to his love. To sing. To be happy in him. Like David sang in Psalm 16:5-6:

Lord, you have assigned me my portion and my cup;
You have made my lot secure.
The boundary lines have fallen for me in
   pleasant places.

Each day is a gift that brings us closer to eternity, when we'll rejoice without ceasing.

My friend didn't have to worry about supplying dinner after an "autopsy." At least not yet. The pathologist concluded the spots weren't cancerous. But now as I work at the kitchen sink, doing what the ordinariness of life asks, I'm refreshed by those verses.

God is teaching me to number my days—not to worry, but to worship the One who created them.

Jeanne Zornes says that being forty-plus *"gives me a good reason for all those wrinkles and my bifocals."* She is a graduate of Western Washington University, Multnomah School of the Bible, and Wheaton Graduate School of Communication. Jeanne has published hundreds of magazine articles and is the author of *When I Prayed for Patience . . . God Let Me Have It!* A frequent conference speaker, she is the mother of Zachary and Inga and the wife of Rich Zornes, an elementary school physical education specialist.

Airport Angel
Rebecca Puntigam

Leader of Pioneer Girls Club
Seattle, Washington

"Well, young man, I see you have your boarding pass, but where is your ticket? I can't give you a seat assignment or let you on the plane without it." The passenger agent pensively eyed my fourteen-year-old son, Joel, and then looked over at me.

I moved up to the counter with my five-year-old daughter Marissa and my sixteen-year-old autistic son Nathan. I hoped I could straighten out the problem with Joel's ticket quickly, but the tense situation became the catalyst to set Nate off into an uncontrollable temper tantrum. As he began to scream and dart away, I had to shift all my attention to him, pulling him down onto the terminal floor where he could not knock anyone or anything over. All I could do was look hopelessly at the agent, leaving Joel's first solo plane trip in question.

The woman came over to talk to me further. Seeing I could be of no help right then, she suddenly announced that although the ticket was missing, surely Joel had checked in properly because he had his baggage claim checks. Therefore, he could get on the plane. I was too busy to do more than quickly thank her and nod good-bye to Joel.

I concentrated on trying to get Nate calm enough to let him stand up so we could successfully leave the airport terminal and get to our car. People walked around us giving us puzzled or concerned glances. A passer-by offered Nate some corn chips. Nate flung them away and continued thrashing his arms and legs. Another adult stopped and helped hold Nate down for a few moments before he apologetically left to catch his plane. In the past, when Nate had gotten out of control in public, there had always been my husband, older children, or another adult I know to help remove Nate to a place where he could calm down. I now felt completely helpless and had no idea what I could do by myself.

This was just the sort of situation I had always dreaded happening. For several years, I had not gone out in public with just Nathan and Marissa. Nate's behavior was just too unpredictable and Marissa was too young to care for herself if Nate ran off. Yet, here we were alone.

This had not been the original plan, of course. After I had gotten the nonrefundable tickets, my husband realized that Joel's departure time conflicted with a seminar he had promised to give. Clark was not able to come to the airport, but we had prayed for God's help and protection while I would be responsible for the children by myself.

There I was, crouched on the floor, holding Nathan down, while Marissa sat beside me with an ashen face. Suddenly, a man was at my side. He was extremely calm and seemed totally knowledgeable about how to handle my situation. He took over with Nate, announcing that he was a fireman and had a mentally challenged brother.

He quickly managed to get Nate upright and moving towards the escalator and the airport subway. I followed with my frightened little girl clinging to my hand. We steadily moved out of the terminal into the parking garage. Although we talked very little, the stranger revealed this was his first time at Seattle International Airport.

Finally Nathan was safely inside the car, though he was wildly kicking everything in sight. The stranger expressed concern over whether I could yet handle my son. I thanked him for his help and assured him that Nate would soon calm down. Marissa and I quickly got into the car. She immediately threw up her breakfast in response to the morning's events. I momentarily forgot the helpful stranger as I cleaned up the mess and drove away.

The phone was ringing when we walked through the house door. It was the passenger agent calling to see how we were. She told us that she could see how worried Joel was at leaving his family at such an upsetting moment, so she had upgraded his seat from coach to first class, where he sat beside another teenage boy. Having a son herself, she knew Joel needed something fun and different to occupy his mind. That serendipity succeeded! Joel was full of his exciting plane experience when he called several hours later, laughing that his brother's handicap sometimes brought good surprises.

Since that summer morning, I have repeatedly reflected on how we were given help to get out of a difficult set of circumstances. God gave us a trusting airline agent who took care of Joel and gave him a better trip than he might have had otherwise. The stranger arrived to help us just when the situation seemed hopeless. Why didn't he have any time restraints? Was he a man whom God had placed just where his special skills were needed? Or was he an angel? I do not know the answer to that question. I do know without a doubt that the Lord protected and rescued us when we were in trouble, just as he promises.

Becky Puntigam says the best part about being forty-plus is that *"I am no longer a slave to fashion and I feel freer to be myself."* She is a graduate of the University of California at Berkeley and helps facilitate Neighborhood Bible Studies. Becky volunteers in the public schools and also is a leader for Pioneer Girls Clubs. She is the mother of Erin, Nathan, Joel, and Marissa and the wife of Clark Puntigam, a patent attorney.

Though you have made me see
troubles, many and bitter, you
will restore my life again;
from the depths of the earth
you will again bring me up.
You will increase my honor
and comfort me once again.
Psalm 71:20-21

Light in the Dark
Cheryl Sanders

Bible Teacher, Soloist, and Pianist
Asheville, North Carolina

Finally the conference was over. Norm and I had planned a three-week vacation in Europe as a reward. How desperately we needed a break after an intense year of ministry in Amsterdam. I couldn't wait!

But when my husband came home that night, he had startling news. "We've been assigned to England for a year. Unfortunately, I need to get started right away so our vacation plans will have to wait."

I was not thrilled.

Because Norm coordinated ministry in a different location every year, I had reached the saturation point from the stress and strain of our nomadic lifestyle. To me it seemed worse than being in the military. We had traveled thirteen of our thirteen years of marriage. Hadn't we paid our dues? I was ready to give it all up in exchange for a home of our own where we could put down roots and enjoy the feeling of being settled.

During the preempted vacation weeks, Norm flew back to the States on business and left me behind in Amsterdam with our three-year-old son and a second child on the way. Disappointed and seething with anger, I realized that there was nothing left to do but grit my teeth and get on with single parenting.

By the time we had moved to England and settled into yet another rental home outside of Birmingham, I had begun to experience panic attacks—episodes that awakened me at night. I didn't think too much about them, since I was usually able to go back to sleep. Nonetheless, the fearful pounding of my heart continued to rob me of rest. These panic attacks left me feeling physically, mentally, and emotionally exhausted.

Needing every ounce of strength to carry my unborn child, I tried to fulfill my daily responsibilities. But I secretly wondered if I was heading for a major emotional and physical breakdown. From sheer determination, I held on to control for the sake of the little life within me. I was afraid to seek professional help. But I did cling to two promises God had given me: Psalm 71:20-21 on the previous page and Psalm 138:7: "Though I walk in the midst of trouble, you preserve my life; you stretch out your hand against the anger of my foes, with your right hand you save me."

Like the prophet, Jeremiah, I felt God was making me dwell in darkness, walling me in so that I could not get out. "I have been deprived of peace; I have forgotten what prosperity is. So I say, 'My splendor is gone and all that I had hoped from the Lord'" (Lam. 3:17-18).

My body continued to scream for sleep and rest. My doctor recommended that I take sleeping pills. Even though I was worried they might harm my baby, I took them out of desperation. Then I'd doze for five or ten minutes only to be awakened by another panic attack. The pills kept me feeling drugged. Was there no end to my misery?

Even God seemed far way. I wondered if he really cared. Those who knew about my illness and wanted to help in some way offered such comments as: "I can't believe that you of all people are depressed," or "Christians aren't supposed to have nervous breakdowns." Needless to say, such well-meaning comments only increased my guilt and depression.

Tired of living with all of the torment and terror of my hellish existence and looking for a way out, I became obsessed with thoughts of suicide. I kept the sleeping pills right at my finger tips. But even though I felt somewhat justified at the possibility of taking my own life, I could never justify taking the life of my unborn child.

I knew that God in his sovereignty had a wonderful plan for this precious life and I couldn't interfere with that plan. I guess I had hope for my child, but not for me. "He has walled me in so I cannot escape; he has weighed me down with chains. Even when I call out or cry for help, he shuts out my prayer. He has barred my way with blocks of stone" (Lam. 3:7-9).

After seven or eight months of hell, I sobbed from desperation, brokenness, and pain, "Norm, I cannot cope any longer!" Then I went upstairs and read this verse from Isaiah: "Who among you fears the Lord and obeys the word of his servant? Let him who walks in the dark, who has no light, trust in the name of the Lord and rely on his God" (Isa. 50:10). My life certainly was dark. But God still wanted me to trust him!

A few minutes later, Norm joined me upstairs, took my hand and began to sob with me and said, "I wish there was something I could do to help you." Like a balm in Gilead, his words and expressions of love began to soothe my troubled soul.

A few nights later, I got up to gaze upon the beautiful autumn moon. I began to focus my attention on God and on the reality of his existence. I was overcome with the energizing truth that God always was and always will be the eternal God who is the same yesterday, today, and forever. It was as if God were saying, "Cheryl, I am your reason for living and I am all that you need to accomplish that purpose, for I am your life. I was with you yesterday, today, and will be with you tomorrow."

His presence that evening and words of assurance became my treasure in the darkness, bringing light and hope to my despairing soul. The eternal God, my refuge, had been carrying me all along in his everlasting arms and would see me through.

This was a beautiful beginning on my long road to recovery. God, in his own way and time, provided a way with the help of professional counselors, doctors, and appropriate medications. Bible reading and prayer became even more meaningful to me as God revealed more of himself in my quest to know him better.

The God who had shown me many troubles and distresses did revive me again with his life and brought me up from the depths of the earth. How I praise him for his faithfulness in fulfilling his promises to me and for giving us a beautiful and healthy seven-pound baby boy during one of the darkest periods of my life. Because I know God is with me in the darkest times and promises to be everything I need, I have confidence to celebrate faith after forty! Truly he is my light in the darkness.

Cheryl Sanders says the best part of being forty-plus is *"seeing God's love, mercy, and faithfulness to me in the past and having the confidence to look to the future."* She grew up singing with the Jones Sisters Trio and studied at Trinity College, Nyack College, and Kent State University. Cheryl continues her ministry of music in addition to mothering Timothy and Ryan. She is married to Norm Sanders, director of public relations at the Billy Graham Training Center at The Cove.

III. MAKING CHOICES

As a high school junior, I was accepted to university and thus faced with a serious decision: Would I stay in high school and enjoy a senior year full of fun and status? Or would I finish my studies that summer and enroll in a college two states away?

I went to college a year early and never regretted it.

Ten years later, after grad school and several years of various work which took me around the world, I was once again faced with a decision: Would I get a job in my beloved Blue Ridge Mountains near friends and family? Or would I accept the call to pioneer a new ministry at a large church near San Francisco?

I moved to California and it changed my life.

Years later, when I prayerfully and gleefully accepted a marriage proposal from a widower with three small children, a friend said to me, "Cindy, you never seem to do things the *easy* way!"

Choices. They make all the difference, don't they? One of my favorite poets, Robert Frost, wrote about two roads diverging in a wood, "And I took the one less traveled by, and that has made all the difference."

I suppose I've spent most of my forty-plus years choosing the road less traveled. But isn't that true of everyone who takes seriously a commitment to live for Christ? The world says move on to greener pastures, Christ says *persevere*. The world says compromise, Christ says *obey*. The world says accumulate, Christ says *sacrifice*.

Midlife is an appropriate time for reflecting back on our choices. Was I ever really that young, that skinny, that naive, and that idealistic? As a seventeen-year-old college freshman, I had told God I would help change the world. I truly believed that I could . . . that we could—together.

Well, Cindy, the world certainly has changed! a little voice in my head smirks. *But probably more in spite of you than because of you. And the change has been from bad to worse. Is that what you had in mind?*

It's odd how time can pass so quickly while we're simply living one day at a time, making choices the best we can. I thought of all the jobs I'd had since college and remembered all the areas I'd lived in. I reflected on the wonderful family I'd gained: husband Michael, children Justin, Timothy, Fiona, and Margaret. I guess I have crammed quite a bit into these past twenty years. But the real question is, has anyone's life been changed due to the choices I've made?

Yes. Mine.

The women you are going to meet in the following pages have also made choices that changed their lives. They, like I, can only hope and pray that somehow along the way, in our feeble efforts to serve Christ and further his kingdom, small seeds have been planted—seeds that have or will bring forth new life in God's timing.

When I first went to college, someone suggested that I choose a life verse to remind me of God's promise and hand on my life. So in 1970, Isaiah 58:10-11 became my life verses. Those words were significant to me then and have remained so through all of life's changes:

> If you spend yourselves in behalf of the hungry and satisfy the needs of the oppressed, then your light will rise in the darkness, and your night will become like the noonday. The Lord will guide you always; he will satisfy your needs in a sun-scorched land and will strengthen your frame. You will be like a well-watered garden, like a spring whose waters never fail.

Yes, there are days when I feel spent and dry in a sun-scorched land. Choices are hard and the well-worn super-highway looks a lot more appealing than the road less traveled. But my Lord has never failed to guide and strengthen. He does indeed quench all thirst.

Many are the plans in a
[person's] heart, but it is the
Lord's purpose that prevails.
Proverbs 19:21

Without Notes
Mary Holder Naegeli

Minister
Moraga, California

It was a joke among my Christian friends in college: "Lord, we'll go anywhere and do anything for you, but please don't send us to Africa!" Why this vast continent would be off-limits in our youthful exuberance is now a mystery to me.

The year I turned forty, I went to Africa. My two daughters, ages thirteen and eleven, accompanied me on a sabbatical leave to Harare, Zimbabwe, where we served the Presbyterian Church for four months. Towards the end of my stay I made some startling discoveries.

Bumping along Zimbabwe's equivalent of a super-highway, I kept my nose buried in a book to avoid seeing the close calls on the narrow, two-lane road. The luxury bus, an extravagant term for a stripped-down version of public transportation, was headed for Masvingo, site of the famous Great Zimbabwe ruins and home to Mucheke Presbyterian Church. The pastor had asked me to make the four-hour journey to meet with a Christian drama group. "Help these twenty talented young people develop skills and find focus for their drama productions, so that we can use them during Sunday worship."

Now *this* was a fascinating assignment! After four months of preaching and singing in eight other Presbyterian churches, after fifteen weeks of teaching weekly Bible studies and conducting an African choir, coaching a drama group was something totally new. And hugging my suitcase under my knees, catching glimpses of the African bush as the sun set in blazing glory, I had no idea what I was going to do for eight hours with people I had never met.

In order to appreciate this scenario, you have to understand something about me: I am by nature Ms. Plan Ahead. I carry a daily planning calendar—my other Bible—with me wherever I go. (My daughters even have their own little daily planners!) I have dates set three years ahead. I write my sermons out word for word. I have been known to start a term paper only two weeks into the quarter. And here I am, hurtling down a Zimbabwean highway without so much as a note to guide me through an imminent and lengthy workshop!

But after fifteen weeks on African time, something was happening to me, and I liked it. Far from being worried about my lack of preparation, I sensed that God was at work in me to be less focused on planning and more focused on participation. I had not been lazy or indifferent. I had given time to working out a plan for this workshop, but realized there were so many unknowns in the situation that it was impossible to determine the appropriate method without meeting the group first.

That night, the deep black faces of Shona preteens, high schoolers, and young adults lit up in the glimmer of candlelight. We shared our stories together. Having no plan to fall back on, no agenda to distract me, I earnestly listened to each story, searching for clues that would help me understand their need and what I could offer.

Around this circle, I discovered in a new way the joy of waiting on the Lord and fully participating with the people around me. It made me wonder how often in the past my plans had actually prevented my participation, how my preconceived assumptions had thwarted a God-breathed inspiration. Since that night in Mucheke, I have viewed preparation for ministry as less the preparation of a *product* and more the preparation of a *person*—me—to be God's instrument, maybe even God's presence, in a given situation.

I suppose about the time a woman turns forty, she begins to recognize the vulnerability of her plans. Some have been fulfilled, but others have been thwarted. Some have been modified by changing life circumstances, and others have been dashed in a moment of tragedy. This has probably been my greatest source of humility: to recognize my deep, deep desire to avoid failure by controlling my future and my humiliating inability to do so. But this humility has become all the more genuine and productive, as God's presence has invaded with power even into my daily planning calender.

By the way, that workshop turned out to be terrific. Though talented and very creative, the young people had yet to discover the possibilities of emotion and movement in their craft. Using the story of the Sabbath healing of the woman bent over since birth (Luke 13:10-17), we explored the feelings of an outcast, how others reacted to her, how Jesus healed her. I enjoyed the fact that Jesus was straightening *me* to stand joyfully in his presence, without a plan but bolstered by his power!

Mary Naegeli believes the best part of being forty-plus is that she has *"accumulated wisdom still appreciated by my teenage daughters."* She is a graduate of Stanford University and Fuller Theological Seminary and serves as a minister at Moraga Valley Presbyterian Church. Mary is also an accomplished soloist and has several recordings. She is the mother of Katy and Judy and the wife of Andrew Naegeli, an electrical engineer.

For through me your days
will be many, and years will
be added to your life.
Proverbs 9:11

Aging Gratefully
Marjorie Wallem Rowe

Writer and Speaker
Osterville, Massachusetts

It was the week before our birthdays. My son Adam was turning eleven, and two days later, I would hit forty. Hitting forty was an appropriate way to describe my mood as we surveyed the rows of paper plates and napkins in the variety store. While Adam was deliberating over whether to choose plates depicting Batman or Power Rangers, I was scanning the lines of adult party goods.

"You're Over the Hill!" trumpeted one paper plate manufacturer, while another reassured me that I was "Aged to Perfection." I shuddered inwardly and turned towards the cash registers with Adam's selections. I was fairly certain that my husband, Mike, would plan some sort of celebration for my fortieth, but I fervently hoped he knew me well enough to know what I did *not* want for my birthday.

I did not want those awful paper products with their inane themes. I did not want an awkward surprise party with 112 of my not-so-close friends. I did not want the inevitable gag gifts: bottles of prune juice, packages of laxatives, and cover-that-gray shampoo formulas. I did not want sympathy. What exactly did I want? I wondered, as Adam and I navigated our way home through the weekend traffic.

Maybe I should ask Mike to skip the fuss altogether, I mused. After all, I was not on a slow decline towards senility, nor was I any closer to perfection than I ever was. None of this forties hoopla for me! I would enter my new decade sedately and with dignity.

Yet I was secretly hoping that my family and friends would remember me. There was nothing worse than saying I didn't need a party and then not getting one! Though I had not yet come to grips with this particular coming-of-age, there was still that *something* about turning forty. Something that deserved at least a little hoopla. Dignity could wait until fifty.

We turned into the driveway and began unloading groceries. Adam ran off to show his dad his birthday paraphernalia. Still mentally planning my perfect party, I flipped through the mail and found an early birthday card from a college friend.

"Look at it this way," the card consoled, "at forty, you're too old to die young!"

"Now that was a cheery thought," I muttered under my breath. *Have I crossed some invisible line in life marked "old"? I've had it with these party goods philosophers*, I inwardly fumed. *I'm up to here with "for women with skin over thirty-five" advertisements. I'm through with birthday cards that make jokes at my expense. I'm through with birthdays!*

The thought hit with an intensity that surprised me. Did I really want to be through with birthdays? Was I so myopic that I couldn't see the obvious flaw in my thinking? How dare I despise this incredible gift from God—a chance to wake up to the world one more day, one more year. A chance that some of my friends from high school and college would never have.

I know what I need for my birthday, I thought ruefully, *I need a little gratitude.*

In his book, *Legacy of Love*, Tim Kimmel reminds us of the importance of being thankful for each new day. "God extends to each of us a timeline of credit," Kimmel writes, "and at any time he can exercise his option to call in the loan."

The aging process carries with it certain regrets. We mourn the loss of the options open to us when we were younger. We become frustrated when our eyesight blurs or our waists thicken. We think wistfully of the days when we could spontaneously drop everything for a weekend bike trip through the mountains.

Unlike the Chinese, who revere their elders, we live in a Western culture that worships youth. It is tempting to slip into the secular mind set of bemoaning our age. Yet our Creator makes it clear that the years he gives his people are a precious commodity to be treated with respect: "Gray hair is a crown of splendor; it is attained by a righteous life" (Prov. 16:31).

French author Victor Hugo expressed it well when he wrote, "Wouldn't it be terrible if we were born old, and had to look forward to growing young, green, and silly?"

This fortyish woman has had quite enough of being young and silly, thank you. God's grace has permitted me to reach a midpoint in life. Unlike Moses, who lived to 120 with his eyes "not weak nor his strength gone," I may suffer infirmities as I age. I may live to lose loved ones and witness a world gone again to war. But I can choose not to long for the past nor fear the future. I can choose to *age gratefully.*

Maggie Rowe rejoices that at forty-plus *"I am coming into myself—becoming more the woman God created me to be, rather than a reflection of others' expectations."* She is a graduate of Wheaton College and works with women throughout New England in her ministry of speaking, conference coordination, drama, and Bible teaching. Maggie is the mother of Adam, Amber, and Jordan and the wife of Michael Rowe, pastor of Osterville Baptist Church on Cape Cod.

I will instruct you and teach
you in the way you should go;
I will counsel you and watch
over you.
Psalm 32:8

He Holds
the Thread

Kerry Dearborn

Professor of Theology
Seattle, Washington

Watching the dashboard clock and urging my car forward in the misty hours of Seattle's clogged morning rush hour, an image of former days in Scotland tugged at my mind. Not long ago at such an hour, I would have been winding along the farm road, which led from our two-hundred-year-old croft, through gentle rolling hills and sleepy pastures, to take our daughters to school in the nearby village.

After dropping them off, I might have stopped by a friend's for coffee and a chat together in front of her warm hearth, or I might have just enjoyed seeing friends and acquaintances in and about the village square before having to dive into my daily routine of study. Though life was full in Scotland, it seemed there was always time for conversations and spontaneity in relationships.

After five years of living in such a haven of natural, quiet beauty and intimate, embracing relationships, how had I come to be here—in this large, busy American city? How had I gone from endless quiet hours of reflection and reading within the parentheses of our daughters' school days and my husband's work, now to be bustling off at 7:30 each morning to face a class, who looked to me to enable growth in their theological understanding? Life in Scotland seemed to be symbolized by the image of the village square or the hearth in our Scottish farmhouse, which continually drew our family and others into its warmth and centeredness (we had no central heating).

In contrast, the symbols of life in a large American city seemed to be the sprawling freeways and endless shopping malls. Questions about all these changes flooded my mind. Perhaps the most puzzling question about my new life was one which surfaced from the echoes of my childhood training: How could I have moved from my place of homemaking (which from birth I had been told was a woman's only place, and for which I had been grateful) to a job as a professor, which forced me to face some of my deepest fears and but also brought me great joy?

It had been much like Princess Irene's pilgrimage following her great-great-grandmother's thread in George MacDonald's *The Princess and the Goblin.* Change had come one step at a time. MacDonald writes of Princess Irene, "Then, to her surprise, and somewhat to her dismay, she found that instead of leading her towards the stair [where her grandmother and the fire of roses could be found], the thread turned in quite the opposite direction." Like the princess, the thread of life had led me out of the safety of my home to many unexpected places. There had been no five- or ten-year plans with lists of short-term goals. Life with a growing family involved too many interruptions and commitments for me ever to have established a long-term life strategy.

Initially, I never dreamed that thread would lead me to complete a doctorate, with all the challenge and wonder of being able to devote five years part-time to engage in theological reading and reflection, especially to be able to focus on the theology of George MacDonald. The thought of actually being led to teach, to begin a "real" job, had seemed such a remote and distant possibility.

When Princess Irene found herself in a fearful cavern, having faithfully followed her grandmother's thread, she reminded herself how kind and beautiful her grandmother was. Discovering that her thread led her straight into a wall of rocks and later into the cave of her gravest enemies, she agonized but held fast to her course, convinced that the other end of the thread was held tightly by the one who loved her and would not fail her.

I know that my life has unfolded as it has, not through my great obedience, but because Jesus holds the other end of the thread, and by his Spirit helps me to hold my end. In the caverns of my self-doubt and feelings of utter inadequacy, his face of gentle love and encouragement urges me on—to trust him with the next step.

Though it leads me into a world of sluggish freeways, immense challenges, and a demanding schedule, the thread will not break or vanish. He leads me on and on, ever drawing me nearer to himself, that I might know: He is my true hearth, whose fire of roses will not only warm and cleanse me, but may eventually even make me fragrant like him.

Kerry Dearborn believes the best part about being forty-plus is *"the richness of our family life together."* She graduated from Whitman College, Fuller Theological Seminary, and holds a Ph.D. from the

University of Aberdeen, Scotland. Kerry currently teaches theology and is the mother of Alison, Andrea, and Bethany. She is married to Tim Dearborn, director of the Seattle Association of Theological Education.

Trust in the Lord, and do good; Dwell in the land and cultivate faithfulness. Delight yourself in the Lord; and He will give you the desires of your heart. Commit your way to the Lord, Trust also in Him, and He will do it.
Psalm 37:3-5, NASB

The Question
Anne Wheeler-Waddell

Minister and Seminary Teacher
Kikuyu, Kenya

"Will you marry me?"

How many times in my almost thirty-nine years of life had I prayed, hoped, dreamed, given up ever hearing those words? In recent years, I had actually grown quite comfortable in my single life as a Presbyterian pastor and mission coworker living and working in East Africa. Now home on an extended leave, engrossed in a graduate study program, and preparing to return in a few months to Kenya, *now of all times,* the question came.

But other questions tumbled forth, too. How does John fit with my sense of call? Kenya is a very patriarchal society. Would John's presence and ministry begin to overshadow mine? Marriage is a calling. Is God calling me, and us, to this? And the small questions—Can I live with this person full-time, twenty-four hours a day, seven days a week? Enjoying my own space, I had not had a housemate for years.

"Will you marry me?"

"Yes, . . . I think so." It took the better part of two months of sorting and praying through the big and small questions to drop the qualifier and simply say yes!

This radical and blessed shift in my life taught me two great lessons—one, about God's faithfulness, and the other, my own faithfulness.

God's faithfulness. At the time I had announced my missionary intent, I could just imagine people sighing and thinking, "Well, I guess you've chosen to go to Africa instead of getting married." It was as if going to rural Kenya was closing the door on any possibility of meeting an eligible mate. For others, my pursuing further graduate studies and training moved me beyond the bounds of any reasonable prospect.

But to those willing to listen, I would express my heartfelt conviction: "If God intends for me to have a life partner, I don't believe I have to move outside of my life's course and calling to find one. God is quite capable of bringing two people's lives together, two people who are moving (or following Christ) in the same direction."

God is able. God is faithful. During my seminary training and first six years in Kenya, God had led John into a military career flying helicopters and next to seminary training for overseas ministry. It was to that same seminary that I returned on furlough and met John in his final year. Only God can work out timing like that!

God is able. God is faithful. We do not have to move outside the path on which he is leading us to find the fullest expressions of his faithfulness.

My faithfulness. Not only is God faithful, but he calls me to a lifetime of faithfulness. The living out of that life has radically changed since marriage. On the one hand, I sometimes say, "God brought John into my life." But it is equally true that God brought me into John's life. How does God want to use me in my husband's life? How do I encourage his calling even as I continue to live out my calling in ministry? How do I live out my faithfulness now in this God-blessed primary relationship?

But it is my faithfulness to the Lord that I'm still working on, even in my third year of marriage. Living alone, it was easy to wake early for times of prayer and study. Living alone, it was easy to pour out my heart and hurts and hopes to God. Now, it is too easy to pour them out to my husband.

Fortunately, John has the wisdom to occasionally let me know I am pouring out in the wrong place and to the wrong person, and he directs me to the Lord. But I am still learning how best to keep my private, alone time with the Lord in the context of shared space and a shared life. Not only is this time needed for my own spiritual health and that of my husband, but it is needful as well because God delights in the intimacy of relationship with me.

Christ never fails to prove his faithfulness. At forty-plus in Kenya, and on visits home to the United States, I delight in sharing life with my partner and fellowship with my Lord. My hope is that I continue to cultivate faithfulness.

Anne Wheeler-Waddell is glad that at forty-plus *"I have some life experiences and years in Christ already behind me and part of who I am."* She grew up in northern California, graduating from Occidental College and earning two master's degrees from Fuller Theological Seminary. Anne enjoys teaching New Testament and preparing African students for pastoral ministry at the Pastoral Training Institute. She is married to John Wheeler-Waddell, a Presbyterian minister and chaplain at Alliance High School.

The Lord will fulfill His
purpose for me; your love,
O Lord, endures forever—
do not abandon the works of
your hands.
Psalm 138:8

Starting Over
Janet Holm McHenry

Author and Teacher
Loyalton, California

I looked at the form in my hands. Huge splotches of water had collected on it from my tears. Ink smeared as I tried to tissue them up.

Great, I thought. *I'm sure National University will be really impressed with this.*

It was my application for a fifth-year teacher credential program. I had decided over the last month to return to college at age thirty-eight to make a career change. For nine years, I had been working for my husband, Craig, as his secretary/paralegal/bookkeeper in his small law office. But it wasn't going to be the rest-of-my-life career. I was just there on a temporary basis, I had told him since the start.

My career had been as a newspaper reporter and city editor for a daily newspaper. Then we moved to Loyalton—a town of twelve hundred people, where the nearest daily newspaper was an hour away in good weather. So I filed away my steno pads and tape recorder and resigned myself to working for Craig—with the promise to myself that someday I would again work for a newspaper.

I *had* to. It was in my blood. I had chased fire engines, bank robbers, and local politicians. I had watched Mt. St. Helens and the Jim Jones stories come over the wires. I had pounded out a hot story at the very last minute and then just an hour later read it on the front page. I couldn't imagine a job more fulfilling!

That was why I was bawling my eyes out as I completed the application. I'd been crying for two full days about this midlife change. It wasn't something *I* had wanted to do. In fact, there were two professions I had always told people I could never do. One was nursing. The other was teaching.

My mom had always urged me to try teaching. She had just retired from teaching after twenty years. It was a change she had made in midlife, as well, to help pay for college expenses. She had survived, but the stories she could tell.

During the fifteen years of our marriage, my husband had also prodded me towards teaching. He felt it could make me available to our kids during their off hours. But I figured he just wanted me to bring home a paycheck so he could do less lawyering and more farming. He had bought our farm four years before and loved driving his tractor and watching the rodents run through the fields. *That's how I feel, God—like a rodent running for her life. Like someone else is making me do something I don't want to do and I'm going further and further away from what I thought I'd be doing with my life.*

Along the way, I realized that what was real in my life was something very different than I had intended. Friends had pointed out my teaching strengths through Junior Church and Sunday school leadership. My pastor had complimented me recently on some presentations I had made. "Have you ever thought of teaching?" he had innocently inquired.

And then God spoke. "Janet, your plans aren't always my plans. I will fulfill my purpose through you and it sure would be easier if you'd decide to cooperate."

So I did. I blew my nose and washed my face. And I decided that was the end of my midlife crisis—all forty-eight hours of it. I sent the application. Soon afterward, I finished the credential program, passing three difficult tests many others did not. And I've been teaching now for five years.

And the strangest thing is I have absolutely no desire to walk into a newsroom ever again—unless I'm taking my school kids on a tour.

Janet McHenry is thankful that at forty-plus *"I know myself and I'm realizing how much God loves me."* She received her journalism degree from the University of California at Berkeley and now enjoys teaching at school and church. Janet has authored many children's books, including the Golden Rule Duo series and the Amazing Stories series. She is the mother of Rebekah, Justin, Joshua, and Bethany and is the wife of Craig McHenry—attorney, farmer, and rancher.

*You knit me together in my
mother's womb. . . . I am
fearfully and wonderfully
made. . . . All the days
ordained for me were written
in your book before one of
them came to be.
Psalm 139:13-14, 16*

What About
the Babies?

Christina Sue Alig Bakker

Counselor and Pro-Life Advocate
Quincy, Illinois

"B*lessed are they that mourn, for they will be comforted."*

Another night awakened in uncontrollable tears! All I
could remember was the same dream of millions of broken
babies crying—crying with no one to care for them. These
were the victims of abortion and my tears were a silent
witness to the intensity of grief coming from somewhere.
But where? Why was I having these dreams?

Abortion had been a topic I had wrestled with intellectually in college and spiritually in my work in the inner
city and a group home for troubled teens. Now I was married to a minister and had four children. In the middle of
the night I went downstairs to pray and ask the Lord why
I was having these recurring dreams.

His answer came back simply and clearly: "The Holy Spirit is grieving the loss of my little ones. You are a vessel of my grief."

I had never heard of anyone being a vessel for God's grief, but I knew this strange ministry was something he was doing and I sought to obey. I answered, "Then, I am your servant, Lord. If I am to be a vessel of your grief, let it be." I always felt God's comfort during those tearful times, knowing the grief belonged to God.

"Blessed are the merciful, for they will be shown mercy."

Within a couple of months, I understood the Lord to be saying it was not enough for me to *know* abortion was wrong; he wanted me to *do* something about it. But the problem seemed overwhelming and I knew no one else who was doing anything about it. So I prayed for God to show me what he wanted me to do. No answer. I fasted and prayed some more.

My life experiences in my twenties and thirties had focused my attention on broken unborn babies and their suffering as victims of abortion. I was given understanding of women who suffer alone with a problem pregnancy. Also, in my counseling practice, I had agonized with clients who bore the impossible guilt and grief of having allowed their child to be destroyed within their own wombs. Only the realized reality of the Cross could lift so heavy a load and make forgiveness of self possible.

But as I continued to wait on him, I guess that God wanted to teach me to be totally reliant on him and not on my past experiences or my own abilities and strengths, because he certainly had some bigger tasks in mind than I could ever have accomplished.

Soon I was given an opportunity to coordinate a seminar for those in the helping professions in a two-state area, to provide resources for helping women and their unborn children in a noncondemning and life-promoting way. It was only in humble reliance on him that the seminar became a reality. Gradually, others in my church began to see the need and began a ministry to unwed mothers in a group home. I enjoyed giving the devotionals there when possible. These personal encounters blessed me to see God's mercy in action.

"Blessed are those who hunger and thirst for righteousness, for they will be filled."

As I neared my forties, a gnawing hunger and burning thirst for God's righteous justice on behalf of pre-born children and mothers in need settled into the core of my soul.

I had to speak, organize, teach, and minister on behalf of women and the unborn. Abortion was no longer sanctioned only in the secular world; even some churches were now endorsing abortion as a moral good!

It is tough to balance family and ministry, and one time I didn't think I should travel to speak because I'd have to leave my family. My children urged me, "But Mom, if you don't go, who will tell the people about the babies? Who will help the mothers who need help?" I went and God supplied grace to my husband and friends to help with the kids. How else is the world going to see any difference? How else will they know hope and healing from the body of Christ?

"Blessed are those who are persecuted because of righteousness, for theirs is the kingdom of heaven."

Because of the stand I have taken for human life, some well-meaning Christians have called me "the radical." But I think all Christians should be known as radicals. Jesus was a radical. And look where it got him. The cross? Yes. Glory? Yes!

It is scary to contemplate losing something if we do the hard thing. But, whoever loses his or her life for Jesus' sake will find it. It is risky to be a radical, but at this point in life, I believe it is more risky *not* to be.

One Sunday, two couples became angry and silently left a discussion group when God's Word was opened on the topic of abortion. Later another couple thanked my husband and me for taking a stand. They confided that they had been plagued with guilt and nightmares after aborting several children prior to marriage. But when exposed to the Word of God, their guilt was validated and the opportunity to be truly forgiven became a reality. They experienced Jesus' forgiveness and the nightmares ceased! In such events I see the kingdom of God made present on earth. And that's worth all manner of persecution.

Christy Bakker is glad to be forty-plus because she has *"new strength and confidence in who the Lord is and how he works through me uniquely, so I can now 'tell it like it is'!"* She is a graduate of Southern Methodist University and holds a master's in counseling from Gordon-Conwell Theological Seminary. Christy is the founder of the Heartland Presbyterians Pro-Life organization, is involved in the Presbyterian renewal movement, and loves to 'invest in the futures' of her four children: Heather, Joshua, Amanda, and April. Her husband, Rodney Bakker, is the minister at First Presbyterian Church.

Grant me a willing spirit,
to sustain me.
Psalm 51:12

Moving to Moscow

Jan Dearman

Missionary in Spiritual Formation
Siberia, Russia

Forty-one and loving it! Why? Because I can still swing with the younger set as a friend and trustworthy mother figure, and I can hang in there with the over-forty set in life's experiences. My niece tells me not to wear those old lady shoes, and another young friend thanks me for being her second mother. Yes, I like being forty-one.

Soon I'll be moving to Moscow to begin a new life. During the past four years of my missionary experience in Hungary, the country became my home. Leaving my adopted country is certainly one of the hardest things I've ever done.

A year ago I was sitting with an older Hungarian friend who is a mother of four, dedicated wife, and full-time geologist. I was gently breaking the news to her that this time next year I would probably be moving to Russia. I saw it as a great challenge that the Lord had opened. Her response caught me totally off guard. "This has to be of Satan. Certainly God wouldn't ask you to leave your physical therapy career in the United States, go to Hungary to learn the language and extend the church, and then ask you to go to Russia. No, this is of Satan."

At that moment I felt fifty-two. This couldn't be happening! Not this Christian lady I had known for four years and in whom I was counting on to pass on her spiritual wisdom to the next generation. But she did have a point.

I had been praying for God to continue to open the opportunities in Moscow. But because of my friend's comments, I began to pray for God's will rather than my own. I had to ask God to judge the motivation of my heart. My friend was right to remind me to seek God's will in the matter so that I wouldn't be deceived by Satan. Honestly, though, it caught me off guard. I had expected my friend to rejoice with me in this next step. I also began praying that God would change the Hungarians' feelings about Russians.

We continued our regular meetings for several months and nothing was said about Russia. During this time my friend went through many struggles at work, with her family, and in her church. God was showing me what I had hoped—this lady was going to do just fine in God's hands when I left.

But one day my friend cried and told me I was the only Christian friend she had and that she would miss me terribly. She offered to help set me up in my apartment in Moscow, taking a thirty-hour train ride which would cost a whole month's wages. She also gave me gifts for Russia. I was astounded! She had a family to care for and she was sacrificing for me.

I reminded her that I wasn't choosing Russia over Hungary and that I still believed it was God's will for me to go. It was, for me, an act of trust and obedience since I was volunteering to learn a new language and move to a colder climate. My friend knew that language studies are particularly hard for me, and that I hate cold weather. We both expressed our sisterhood in Christ and what it costs to be a disciple.

She was paying a high price—she had to let go of me while her world would stay relatively the same. On the other hand, God had already been preparing me to let go and move to a new world hoping to fill that void with new friends. We cried many tears of joy as we prayed together. I sensed the Lord teaching us about his love and our response in faithful love back to one another. He did it in his way in his time.

It has been my custom to spend my birthday with that particular Hungarian family. I always would tell them I'm glad to be getting older because it signifies getting closer in my journey home to be with the Lord. They always smile politely. So I have promised that as often as I can, I'll still return each December and spend my birthday with this family. "Not by might, nor by power, but by my Spirit, says the Lord"(Zech. 4:6).

I'm constantly seeing new mercies every morning and in every relationship. Only time will tell what God had in mind from all this. My job is to joyfully follow his voice one step at a time in the direction he leads, and faithfully obey all that he asks of me. God is continually working his purposes out as he grows me up. It is my heart's desire to follow him all the days of my life.

Ah, . . . forty-one and still growing!

Jan Dearman is glad to be forty-plus because *"I'm closer to heaven because I'm halfway through life!"* She is a graduate of the University of North Carolina and holds a master's in physical therapy from the University of Alabama. Jan serves on the field staff with Church Resource Ministries, and after a year of service in Moscow, now works in Siberia.

*"For I know the plans I have
for you," declares the Lord,
"plans to prosper you and not
to harm you, plans to give
you hope and a future."*
Jeremiah 29:11

Trade-Offs
Laurie Hiller Brumbaugh

Mother and former Pastor
Englewood, Colorado

"I know the plans I have for you . . ."

Yes, but I don't know them. At twenty I waited for signs, for some hands-on type of direction from God. *Just show me; I'll do it.* At forty, I realize the pain and agony of making a decision. Robert Raines talks about "going out not knowing." Every decision feels like a risk, and means all that is not chosen is lost.

Trade-offs is a code word I have discovered used by most of us in the second half of life. But this has been a rough discovery for me because I thought I'd have it all together by the time I reached the big you-know-what.

Trade-offs. At twenty-nine, when I was blessed with my first child, I thought I could continue my pastoral duties as if nothing had changed. I did for a while, because my husband and I shared one job and shared child care.

By age thirty-four, I was the mother of three and it had become harder and harder for me to have it all. The demands of the pastorate were too similar to the administrative and emotional demands of running a home. So, after the third baby, that "still, small voice" began calling me to leave my job and be home for a time.

I obviously considered the risks involved tremendously scary, because it took me two years to act on that voice. *Who would I be if not a pastor?* I thought. How would "my" people survive? What would people think? How would my worth be measured? Would God love me if I were not serving the church?

I began to realize that my identity as a pastor had become all-important. As I let go of that identity, further realizations would follow. Such as discovering I had gone into ministry as much to meet my own needs as I did to help others. The theme of my preaching had always been "God's unconditional love." Deep down I realized I didn't believe it myself for a minute! Oh, I did intellectually, but emotionally, mine was a system of constant bartering with God. Gordon Fee, a New Testament professor, used to describe the Pharisees as holding a trump card of good works so that God would have to accept them as righteous. My biggest trump card was my service to God's people.

Letting go of this involved grief, loss, confusion, and fear. There was much throughout my life I had never been allowed to grieve or feel. But in the letting go also came healing, new discoveries, and great joy. Perhaps the second half of life has to do with learning to move through our losses, and meet God there in a new way. It seems so for me.

In ministry there are few outside sources of "job well done." In parenting and running a home there are *none*. No one will even notice if I stay in my pajamas all day today! And yet, as I have realized the depth of my love for my children, I have seen God as a parent whose love does not depend on what I do, but on who I am (whether or not I even know who I am).

My first baby is as tall as I am, or will be shortly. Some days seem endless, especially when my two-year-old (our fourth blessing) is being two! I know, though, that all too soon, the house will be quiet and I'll miss them all. Occasionally I feel a stirring within of what else I may be called to do. It has no form yet, only ideas and feelings. I assume that when it is time, it will become clear.

Right now, I hear my two-year-old yell "Mom?" with a panic in her voice that says she's lost without me, and I again affirm that "call" for today.

Laurie Brumbaugh says the best part of being forty-plus is *"being through with the twenties and thirties and taking up my own space!"* She is a graduate of Simmons College and Gordon-Conwell Theological Seminary. As an ordained Presbyterian minister, Laurie has served on several presbytery committees and received an award from the town of Islip, New York, for her contribution to women in religion. Laurie is mom to Matthew, Jonathan, Sarah, and Jenny and is the wife of David Brumbaugh, minister of Presbyterian Church of the Covenant.

I tell you the truth, whatever
you did for one of the least of
these brothers of mine, you
did for me.
Matthew 25:40

Fulfilling
a Dream
Susan McDonald Wood

School Principal
Sevierville, Tennessee

As my husband fell to his knees in a prayerful position, my heart stopped for a moment. He was on the phone, obviously prodding the other person to continue expounding upon the topic they were discussing. As I moved near him to get a read on what type of news he was getting, he signalled for me to pray and so I did. Jim listened attentively for what seemed to me like a very long time. I could tell it was not a family emergency, but rather some promising opportunity. However, I was not prepared for the news.

Since before our marriage, we had prayed continually that God would make a way for us to start a ministry for children needing a home. Now Jim was hearing about a possible land donation for it to really happen! The woman who had called was in contact with a group that was planning to donate one hundred acres for ministry to children and families.

She felt a strong prompting to tell her pastor, but was reluctant to do so. She had only recently joined the large, affluent suburban Atlanta congregation and couldn't understand the urgency to tell Jim about an opportunity which seemed so unrelated to his busy pastorate. But after a month of resisting the urge to call him, she decided to risk embarrassment rather than possibly miss a very important direction from the Holy Spirit.

We scrambled to make a presentation to the board, which controlled the land, just one week later. Three months later they decided our ministry was what God had in mind for their property. While we were elated at the obvious work of God in this provision, we were also very happily ensconced in a comfortable, growing pastorate. We had a beautiful home. Our boys participated in the spiritual, musical, and athletic opportunities our church afforded. Jim decided on a plan to be the chairman of the board of our new ministry in Tennessee, while remaining senior pastor in Atlanta.

But after three blocked attempts to find the right person to launch our new ministry, we recognized what God was telling us. One of the people who we most wanted to do the job gave us wise counsel. She said, "You will never be able to find someone who is competent to carry out your vision who would be satisfied to carry out someone else's vision."

We had to decide whether or not we really believed God was behind this burden and vision. When our sons heard we were sensing God telling us to launch a new ministry with no promise of a salary or even a place to live, our middle son, Clayton (eleven at the time), responded: "Mom, what is it the Bible says about this? 'A man who doesn't provide for his family is worse than'. . . a what?"

Even though Jim had always been convinced that he would know God's time and the place for the project, I was scared when he decided to risk it all and obey God. But God's provision was more wonderful than we could have imagined.

We've been at Wears Valley Ranch for almost three years now. We have fourteen students, a boys' home, a girls' home, office buildings, a school building, and a guest cottage. God has sent all of the money in project by project. We have kept our pledge to remain debt-free.

In addition, we were able to purchase land and build our own home on land that adjoins the ranch. We have had to learn to trust God day by day and that can often be hard. We've lived through some tough circumstances, but we see God's faithfulness daily.

As Jim is fond of saying, "Having ten million dollars could not possibly give us the security of knowing that our God will provide all of our needs." And if you could see the children—there really is no greater privilege than ministry to *"the least of these."*

Susan Wood is glad at forty-plus to *"have a fully developed identity and a clear sense of calling."* She graduated from Mississippi State University. In addition to her role as principal at St. Andrew's School at Wears Valley Ranch, Susan is the mother of Paul, Clayton, and Andrew and the wife of James Wood, executive director of Wears Valley Ranch and pastor-at-large of Mt. Vernon Baptist Church.

Yet this I call to mind
and therefore I have hope:
Because of the Lord's great
love we are not consumed,
for his compassions never fail.
They are new every morning;
great is your faithfulness.
I say to myself, "The Lord
is my portion, therefore I will
wait for him."
Lamentations 3:21-24

New Every Morning

Marta D. Bennett

Professor and University Dean
Nairobi, Kenya

"So what are you going to talk about next week with the students?" asked a friend. I had been wrestling for weeks trying to select a topic for the late-night student-led worship service on the college campus where I serve as Director of Campus Ministries. What can I say to these young people as I prepare to leave this place? What wisdom can I impart? Or do they care?

After serving at Seattle Pacific University for a number of years, I'll soon be moving to Kenya. There I will join the faculty of Daystar University in Nairobi, teaching and working with students as they grow in depth of faith and life in Jesus Christ.

In some ways, nothing will change; I will continue teaching and working with university students during formative years. In other ways, nothing will stay even remotely the same.

As I think of leaving, it seems as if it were only yesterday when I joined the staff here, yet it was more than twelve years ago. As I was getting my feet on the ground here at the "mature" age of twenty-nine, many of these students were squirming and exploring activities in their first-grade classrooms. Now, twelve years later, as I lean over to look in the mirror, I see flecks of silver in my hair. Twelve years ago the sky was the limit for those eager young first graders. Twelve years later, these students know that space shuttles can explode, families can split, and though Berlin walls can come down, Gulf Wars, Rwandan tragedies, and guns in high schools are far too imminent. What can I say to them when life is in flux, and when the only constants are change and the unexpected, whether for good or for ill?

I twiddled my pencil and absentmindedly began humming a familiar hymn. The words began to surface:

Great is Thy faithfulness, O God my Father;
There is no shadow of turning with Thee.
Thou changest not. Thy compassions, they fail not:
As Thou hast been, Thou forever wilt be.

Great is Thy faithfulness! Great is Thy faithfulness!
Morning by morning new mercies I see;
All I have needed Thy hand hath provided—
Great is Thy faithfulness, Lord, unto me!

That was it. That is what I needed to share with them. Though students are constantly in flux, there is one constant which will never change. Though their parents divorce, and their current "significant other" dumps them for a new love, or they lose a job and face a mountain of school debt, God's faithful presence will never crease.

It is not that God magically waves a wand and all the troubles disappear. No, the passage from Lamentations on which that hymn is based was written out of the groanings and despairs of great affliction. Yet it was out of such adversity that the ancient prophet Jeremiah pronounced the certainty of God's unchanging faithfulness.

Though I am leaving all that is familiar to put down roots in a part of the world I have only visited, I can know that God goes before me preparing the way. Though I am leaving the security of a position, including predictable income, and though I have no idea where I will be living or who will be there for support and fellowship, I have great confidence in the God who promises never to forsake me.

With this in mind, I can proceed into this transition with a sense of wonder and anticipation. As I wake up each new Kenyan morning, I know that I can be confident of the fresh mercies which will await me each day, just as I found them daily here at home.

God's mercies will never be withheld. Even if or when we are tempted to run away to hide, the Lord lovingly seeks us out and finds us. His compassions are never-failing. He is with us, never leaving us. Even in crises, brokenness, or uncertainty, God's hand is there outstretched, ready to steady us, ready to embrace us, and ready to lead us on the way through. Great is God's faithfulness, now and forever. In that is our anchor and our hope.

Marta Bennett says the best part of being forty-plus is *"the wealth of friendships and life experiences—with* *the hope of many more to come!"* She is a graduate of Lewis and Clark College, Fuller Theological Seminary and holds a doctorate in educational leadership from Seattle University. Marta has been listed several times in "Outstanding Young Women of America" and "Who's Who in the West." Currently she teaches and serves as dean of students at Daystar University in Nairobi, Kenya.

A Change of Heart
Francie Griffin Milligan

Missionary Wife and Mother
Marseille, France

It was the third time I had contacted the doctor. The other two times had been face-to-face visits to his office. This time I was mailing a letter from overseas. This time I was not vacillating; the intent of my heart was clearly focused.

Three years had passed since my tubal ligation. I was thirty-nine years old and finally sure I wanted to have my tubes put back together—whether or not I had another child. I knew my body clock was ticking, but that unstoppable clock was not my major concern. Mainly I wanted to turn forty and be at peace with God.

It had all seemed so right and logical. I had prayed and sought the Lord's will. At that time I had acted in faith, following the advice of doctor, family, and friends and had the tubal at thirty-six. We all acquiesced to the often-quoted statistics indicating higher risks in childbearing after the age of thirty-five.

At that time my husband and I were missionaries living in a Muslim country. We had two very young daughters and I was approaching forty. I already knew the stress and strains of living overseas. Raising two daughters with our changeable lifestyle was challenging enough and the decision seemed right at the time.

But I also acted out of fear. I was afraid of being in the high-risk category for another pregnancy in a third world country. At that time we were relocating to a new city and the political situation in the country was unsettling. What if the next child wasn't healthy and normal? Why not stop with our two precious daughters? A child with special needs would probably require leaving our work overseas.

Almost immediately after the tubal I began to regret the decision. To that point, I had always confronted my decisions head-on. The repercussions of decisions had not been traumatic. But I was not prepared for the psychological reaction and emotional battle after the procedure. The regret of using such a definitive form of birth control overwhelmed me. I felt trapped, with no way out. I was consumed with guilt.

I concluded that I had acted more out of fear than out of faith in God. "Everything that does not come from faith is sin" (Rom. 14:23). What had begun as a very pragmatic decision had become a crisis of faith. The issue was not so much the decision itself, but rather the motivation for making that decision.

Ironically, during those three years of turmoil and emotional confusion, the Lord gently showed me how much he was in control—and how unfounded my fears and doubts had been. The political changes in the country that I had dreaded for several years occurred very rapidly and nonviolently. On a personal level, I often met or heard about high-risk women in their forties having babies. God was reminding me of his lordship in all areas of my life.

The decision to write the doctor and arrange reconstructive surgery was a turning point. I had no guarantees that my ability to conceive would be any different after the surgery, but it was my way of clearing my conscience.

After the surgery, I felt a tremendous sense of peace and faith. My confidence was renewed that the Lord was in control of everything that touched my life. He also renewed my faith to confront whatever risks or sacrifices that might be necessary.

God gave me deeper spiritual insight during the three years my tubes were tied. He showed me how I had wanted to manipulate the events and circumstances of my life, as well as how unsettling that process can be.

It has been six years since I posted that letter to the doctor. After three miscarriages, I did give birth to our third daughter at age forty-two. The fabric of my life keeps changing, but the precious lessons of faith and trust in God learned at the threshold of my forties are still with me.

This experience has helped me be more sensitive to other areas in my life where logic and pragmatism can override faith and trust in God's plan for me. Today I'm deeply thankful for the continued sense of peace and confidence he has given. It's good to be forty-five and at peace with God.

Francie Milligan says that her forty-plus years have brought *"a security and acceptance of my place in life and real joy in my relationships in Christ with family and friends."* She holds degrees from Florida

Presbyterian College and Wheaton Graduate School. Francie and her husband, David Milligan, serve as missionaries with Arab World Ministries. They are the parents of Elisabeth, Rebecca, and Laura.

*For we live by faith,
not by sight.*
2 Corinthians 5:7

Showing Up at Mother Teresa's

Lynn Bolte Samaan

Associate Dean
Rockport, Massachusetts

Although it was only 3 A.M., the sultry night air assaulted us with its oppressive heat. So this is Calcutta, I mused as I stepped off the Air India jet, glancing at my friend and traveling companion, Harriett. Her apprehensive look told all. We were bone weary from the fifteen-hour flight, leaving little resources to cope with overly aggressive porters anxious to earn a rupee, custom officials' demands, and armed military men confiscating cameras which dared to snap photos within the airport.

Our journey of faith was now underway.

The call from God had seemed so clear months earlier. We were to seek out Mother Teresa as a role model of Christ's love in action among the poorest of the poor. Harriett had worked hard to find enough material to write a term paper on this woman of God for a seminary course, and we had both done our best to locate her address and plan wisely for this trip. However, all attempts to secure the address of Mother Teresa were in vain and the letter we wrote to the brothers in Calcutta produced no reply.

And so, here we were at Calcutta's airport, with instructions from an Indian friend not to get into a taxi until we'd learned the money and system. We had no address and no assurance it was possible to do what we'd come to do. Our one charge by our mentor and professor Dr. Christy Wilson—to make our primary focus a prayer ministry—was already in progress as we prayed for the Belgium girl in the seat next to ours.

"Is someone here to meet you?" inquired our new Belgium friend after we'd helped her through customs. When she found we expected no one, she offered, "Do come with me. My uncle is a Jesuit and I know he will be happy to take you to Mother Teresa." Soon we were driving down a palmtree-lined road in a jeep, passing throngs of people who were up and about their business at the first glow of morning light.

After waving good-bye to the priest and his niece, who had been God's wonderful provision for us, we turned to face the door of the Mother House, wondering what sort of reception we would get. Would the sisters welcome the American seminarians who were arriving unannounced? I pulled the rope of the bell which tinkled inside a courtyard. The next moment a young Indian sister in a white sari with the blue border answered the door, followed by a European woman about our age. She graciously encouraged us to follow the European to the YWCA for lodging (we must have looked awfully tired) and to return for mass at 6 A.M. the next morning. We later learned that we were immediately viewed as a direct answer to their prayers for English teachers for their novices!

Mass in the morning was accompanied by a wonderful sense of God's presence as we took off our shoes and knelt beside the sisters on the hard floor of the chapel. A crucifix on the wall had the words written next to it, "I thirst." I pondered the impact of this daily reminder that the cups of water given to the poorest of the poor throughout the day were being given directly to the Lord himself.

When the service was over, the sisters went about their work of washing their saris in the courtyard while we waited patiently in the small room to speak to the sister in charge. "Please, would it be possible to sit in on one of your classes instructing the sisters on how you see Christ in the poor?"

The sister smiled and nodded. She then led me to a dimly lit room filled with novices in their late teens and early twenties. I sat down waiting for the class to begin. The shy sisters also waited and finally, awkwardly stood up and, bowing to me, palms together in Indian fashion, said, "Good morning, sister."

"Good morning," I replied, waiting for another long minute. Then the thought struck me—*They are expecting me to teach the class!* Slowly I stood to my feet and asked what page of the book they were studying. The chapter the student showed me was titled "Conjunctions." My mind promptly went blank and I wondered, *Lord, what are you doing?* Midway through the class I confused conjunctions with contractions and was relieved when the bell rang announcing the end of the class. Breathing a sigh of relief, I hardly noticed two of the novices approaching me. "Please, sister, please pray that I might be holy." Then they slipped out the door as silently as they had approached.

I found myself nodding, but inside I was shouting after them, *No, you've got it all wrong. You should be praying for my holiness!* No one had ever requested that of me before. Holiness, I mused, while the impact sunk deep, planting a seed of yearning. Yes, Lord, I want this trip to be for me the beginning of inner transformation into holiness.

Our pattern was quickly established. In the mornings we taught English and in the afternoons God led us as volunteers with the sisters or to meet key Christian leaders in the city. But our prayer ministry took precedence and we often remarked, "I feel like we are merely walking through something that was prepared for us long ago. There must be a deeper purpose in all of this than we realize."

Before long I caught what we affectionately called the "Calcutta shuffle" and was sick as a dog. Harriett, a registered nurse, cared for me and by morning I was better, though still a bit weak and feverish. It was recommended that I rest that day. When Harriett returned from the Mother House she shared with me about a doctor's wife she met there who was very lonely. We then prayed for the Missionaries of Charity, the people we were meeting at the YWCA, and also asked the Lord to minister to that woman in her loneliness.

I felt good the next day, so we decided to visit another hospital and home for the mentally challenged called "Prem Dam." The midday sun beat upon us as we made our way past street vendors, water buffalo, children at play, rickshaws, and overcrowded double decker buses. Stopping an older woman we inquired, "Excuse me, where is Prem Dam?" The woman motioned for us to wait, then disappeared through a gate in the wall. We waited, feeling foolish as the time passed.

Finally, the gate reopened and we were instructed to follow her. Wondering about the wisdom of following this stranger, we hesitated, then turned into the inner courtyard, across it into a house, up a flight of stairs, down a hall, and into a living room. There she motioned for us to sit. We sat, wondering what would happen next. A minute later she reappeared, serving us a cup of tea.

This was getting more interesting by the minute. What was the meaning of all this? I was totally unprepared for the welcome which followed. The doctor's wife we had prayed for the day before entered the room exclaiming how thrilled she was when her servant announced two sisters from the convent had come to her home for a visit! That afternoon God used us to answer our own prayers—we ministered to the doctor's wife in her loneliness.

So much happened that summer. But, even so, one day I said, "Harriett, we have only a few days left and I'm not sure we've grasped the lessons God sent us here to learn."

An hour later, we were back at the Mother House, pouring out our hearts to the sister in charge. "The needs and problems are so vast and devastating. We thought we'd be more changed by now. It's all too much to process."

She smiled and said with a calm reassurance, "Don't worry. You'll be different. You'll know because your prayer life will be different. My recommendation for you is to spend time during your last days here getting to know one of Calcutta's poor very well. That way, when you look back upon this time in years to come, you will not think of statistics, but rather of a human being you know and love, and that will break your heart and make all the difference. You see, Mother tells us, 'You change the world one person at a time.'"

We left, determined to meet our poor person. Our wait did not last more than a block or two when a boy about the age of six came up to us asking for *baksheesh*. Deciding this was the person God would have us befriend, we knelt down to chat. His name was Metaphor. That evening we learned from folks at the YWCA about Calcutta's beggar system through horrific stories of children being intentionally maimed so they would elicit more pity and bring in more income. Theirs was a life of humiliating, inhuman treatment—locked into a system without hope of escape. Our hearts did begin to break, just as the sister had said.

Just one year later, we were able to get one beggar boy from Bangladesh out of the system and into a loving home, good school, and vibrant church—bringing much joy to his adopted family in Oregon.

Bittersweet good-byes were exchanged with our pupils and they even gave us a surprise farewell party. But then we were told the Superior of Education wanted to see us. Minutes later a stern-looking older sister approached announcing, "We just found out yesterday that you are from a Protestant seminary."

My heart sank. All of the sharing of my faith in the classroom was found out and I braced for the scolding. But, instead she said, "If we had known that when you arrived, we would have asked you to teach us the Bible! Is there any way you could return and help?"

I shared this story with students at a chapel service at the seminary soon after my trip. Afterwards, a student came up to me saying God had spoken to her during chapel and she felt she was to accompany me back to Calcutta the following summer. All I could say was, "He did? You are?"

To my amazement, this same occurrence repeated itself again the next day and a few days after that and again and again until by November there were forty students all eager for a life-changing trip to Calcutta! I felt like Mary at Jesus' birth, who could only ponder in her heart these unexpected events and surrender them back to her Lord.

The next summer, with a team of twenty-five, I once again braved the sweltering heat as I disembarked in Calcutta; only this time it was a homecoming. As a team, we had a prayer ministry, served the poor, took sick team members to the hospital, and watched in awe as each journey of faith and transformation unfolded.

To my surprise, not long after our return to the States, I was approached by the seminary asking if I would consider staying on to develop this program as a permanent part of the curriculum. I was dumbfounded, but something deep within witnessed, "This is of God." And despite feelings of inadequacy, for the next four years I poured my life into developing the Overseas Missions Practicum, a two-course program which immediately branched into multiple parts of the world.

During this time, I watched one hundred students embark on missions of prayer, faith, and service among the poor in various parts of the world. My vocation was being shaped; my skills honed. My quest for deep spirituality was launched!

Years later, as wife and mother thousands of miles away from where it all began, I take comfort in knowing the missions program has continued on, shaping the lives of another generation of church leaders. I, too, was still drawing upon my experience in Calcutta as I shaped two other missions training programs in California. Somewhere within my heart, however, the longing to return never left me. Maybe the next time I will really understand all the lessons—and in the process become a little more holy.

Today I am fifteen years older, using different concepts like "spiritual pilgrimage," "prayer walking," and "power ministry." But I don't know what God is doing any more now than I did on that first journey. I only know that we are called to show up and let God be God as he continues to unfold his purposes for us.

Lynn Samaan is glad at forty-plus to see *"convergence in my work, stability as a family, growing spiritual maturity and a better knowledge of myself."* She holds a nursing degree from Columbia University and master's degrees from Gordon-Conwell Theological Seminary and Fuller Theological Seminary. Lynn currently serves as a dean at Gordon College and has been a contributing author to several books, including *Christian Relief and Development*. She is the mother of Rebecca and the wife of John Samaan, president of the Boston Rescue Mission.

IV. GRIEVING OUR LOSSES

The time had come and I knew it. Only I didn't really want to say good-bye. It was autumn in the mountains of Montreat, North Carolina, and I should have been enjoying God's palette of color. My sisters and I had finished packing up my parents' retreat home, which they had just sold to simplify their lives. Soon I would fly home to Connecticut. But there was still one more thing to do.

I borrowed a car and drove out to the little country cemetery on a beautiful hillside. I had never visited a grave site before, but I knew I couldn't close the chapter on my life in Montreat until I said good-bye to Jill. I wasn't prepared for the sobbing and flood of memories that overtook me as I crouched beside the grave and read her name.

Jill and I had met in 1975, two young single women embarking on exciting careers and ready for all life had to offer. We were inseparable for a while. But then I went away to graduate school, she got married and had children, and then later I did the same. All this time we kept praying for one another.

Ten years later, Jill was diagnosed with a brain tumor—the same kind that took her mother's life in her early thirties. Even though Jill's prognosis wasn't good, she lived seven more years. I had moved back to Montreat with my family and was able to assist Jill in some ways. I'd like to say that I treasured every moment spent with her, but actually, every time we got together, I wanted more. Our lives were busy, and then I moved away again.

I couldn't go to Jill's funeral in 1992 due to a prior speaking commitment to a group of business and professional women. But I knew Jill would want me to put forth God's Word. I did, and several gave prayers of commitment that day. I didn't make it back to North Carolina for six more months. My good-byes had to wait. Of course, that made it harder to realize she was really gone.

Until the moment I sat at her grave. I kept talking to her out on that hillside and then laughing at myself because I knew she wasn't there, but in heaven with her Lord. I could almost hear her laughing, too. It was a bittersweet moment. I didn't stay long. I had cried and remembered enough in the intervening months. It was enough.

Perhaps one of the most transforming realities we have to face as adults is our own mortality. For most of us that comes as quite a shock when someone our own age dies suddenly. It seems too soon somehow. Like life is out of sync.

This shock first came to me at age twenty-nine when my former college roommate, Chris, was killed in an automobile accident. She left behind her husband, six-month-old daughter, and a renowned reputation as a psychology professor. I basically couldn't handle it. So I left work and drove up the northern California coastline to Muir Beach, where I found a small bed-and-breakfast. I stayed for two days, grieving and seeking to find some meaning in an event that seemed meaningless.

Eventually, I had to go on living. So did Chris's husband; so did Jill's children. And so did my husband, Mike, when his first wife died of liver cancer fifteen years ago. Psychologists say that when we lose a loved one, *we must grieve*. We grieve sooner or later, but we *will* grieve. If it's put off until later, our grief sometimes bursts out in totally inappropriate ways and at inopportune times.

In this section you will meet women who have faced grief and come through on the other side. They are not ashamed of their tears. In growing older we learn that each loss takes a part of us that will never be wholly restored. But each loss also brings something new—a recognition of the fragility of life; the warning not to waste time; and a better understanding of God's comfort, which we can then pass along to others in grief.

Experts observe that it is rare for a couple to stay married after the death of a child—the stresses are just too great and tend to pull them apart. Is it also rare for believers in Christ to keep the faith after a tragic loss? Perhaps. We rarely have the ability to control the losses of our lives. But we always have the ability to control our response to life's losses.

Even though our faith is tested and many questions go unanswered, it *is* possible to embrace the God of all comfort even tighter after such an experience! These women can help show us how.

And we know that in all
things God works for the
good of those who love him,
who have been called
according to his purpose.
For those God foreknew
he also predestined to be
conformed to the likeness
of His Son.
Romans 8:28-29

Nothing Is Wasted

Lynne Alexander Drake

Church Women's Ministry
Norcross, Georgia

"Your husband's brain tumor was highly malignant," Dr. Johnson told me as he emerged from seven hours of neurosurgery. "Glastioblastomas are not kind tumors. We removed eighty percent of the tumor, but much of it was fingering and could not be removed. I suggest radiation therapy, but frankly, I think he has less than two years."

It was 1978. Terry had just celebrated his twenty-eighth birthday and our first child, Erin, was one month old. Life came hard for this handsome, bald, retired Naval officer, long ago having hung up his wings as a flight instructor in Pensacola, Florida. The seizures, nausea, vomiting, and headaches were all too frequent visitors—signs of the killer enemy silently at work.

Three years later in 1981, Terry celebrated his thirty-first birthday with further surgery to remove more tumor growth. During the chemotherapy, our second daughter Jenna was born into a sad, tense home. By the end of 1982 death released Terry from a long night of struggle. It brought him freedom from pain and suffering, and a new life with his Lord. It brought just the opposite to his thirty-year-old widow. Dragging me in its wake, my husband's death left me exhausted, numbed, and greatly wounded.

Terry and I had committed our lives to God, and many times during those four-plus years of Terry's battle God's sustaining grace was evident. We were set financially, had strong support from those who loved us, and Terry had many good days. But mentally the struggle wore Terry down, and he could be hard to live with. On top of caring for two little ones, I was drained that last year from Terry's poor health. By the time he died I felt like a walking empty shell.

About six months after his death, my faith in God began to teeter. I felt my solid rock beginning to quake. Questions rose within me for which I had no answers. I felt defenseless as the waves of depression and pain rose higher around me. All I felt was hurt. I did not feel my sustaining God. He was gone.

If I could hurt that much *with* God, my agony without him could be no worse. So I told God in painful anger to leave me alone! How could this God who loved me so much bring such sorrow in my life? Knowing he was the only one who could heal Terry, why did he refuse? Something had certainly gone terribly amiss.

I filled spiral notebooks over the months, journaling about my trapped, angry pain. Near the one-year anniversary of Terry's death, deep thoughts of suicide pulled at me. I resented Erin and Jenna's lives because they meant I had to live, and I gladly would have not. Knowing the day would come when even that knowledge would not stay my hand, I finally sought professional help.

I told Dr. Trotter I didn't want him to talk about God. He agreed. Then slowly, over the next eighteen months, in two-steps-forward-one-step-back fashion, my vision began to clear. But as God used Dr. Trotter to help bring this wayward, lost lamb back to his fold, he also had some surprises.

Two and a half years into widowhood, I went through my own brain surgery for a tumor on my pituitary gland and four months later for a cyst on an ovary. God was serious about getting my attention, and I was taking notice!

He also brought someone else into my life—Philip Drake, who wanted to marry me and be a father to my little girls. Truly that was all God's doing! I was still a mental mess, but Phil told my parents he saw potential. We were married in October 1985 and he has been an anointing of oil—God's direct blessing upon my head. Since then God has blessed us further with two little boys.

A few years ago, as I was reflecting back on what God had done in my life, I was brought up short to realize in awe and wonder that the words of Romans 8:28-29 really are true! God took every bit of that valley I had struggled through and worked it for good in my life. As my mother has said, "God doesn't waste anything." This is only possible because he is a sovereign God who is perfect in wisdom.

I now feel nothing but gratitude to God—that he, loving me and seeing me as one called to his good purpose, would allow pain to come my way and use it as an instrument to conform me to the likeness of his Son.

That is sovereign love.

Lynne Drake rejoices in the *"wisdom, confidence, and contentment that come with forty-plus years."* She enjoys working at her church with the women's ministry and the newsletter. Lynne has a degree in elementary education and is the mother of Erin, Jenna, Matthew, and Stephen. She is married to Phil Drake, director of a health care systems company.

She brought an alabaster jar
of perfume, and as she
stood behind him at his feet
weeping, she began to wet
his feet with her tears.
Luke 7:37-38

Big Girls Do Cry
Marjorie Wallem Rowe

Women's Ministries Coordinator
Osterville, Massachusetts

In the middle of a particularly eloquent moment, tears pooled in the eyes of our conference speaker, "I am *not* crying! My eyes are just leaking!"

Her apology of sorts reminded me of one summer when I had confronted my employer about a particular problem. I was earnest in my explanations but he was clearly uninterested. I was adamant, he was bored. Tears of rage and indignation began to form. He glanced at me in disdain and dismissal, "Women!" he snorted. "Tears are for babies. Grow up!" No wonder we feel like we have to apologize for our emotions.

We've grown up in a culture where children taunt each other on the playground by jeering "Crybaby!" Males are told early on that "big boys don't cry." In both sexes, tears and emotions are often seen as a sign of weakness, immaturity, and vulnerability.

Research demonstrates that women cry at least four times as often as men, and that there is a clear correlation between hormones and tear production. Prolactin, the hormone that regulates the production of breast milk, is also present in tears. Since women have a much higher level of prolactin than men, researchers suggest that women are biologically better producers of tears.

Biologically accepted, yes; socially accepted, no. In order to compete in a man's world, we are taught that it's best not to act too typically female. Being tough and assertive is in; being soft and feminine is out. "Big girls" don't cry either.

Yet the familiar passage in Ecclesiastes tells us that there *is* a time to weep. The apostle Paul showed emotions when he wrote to the Corinthians, "out of great distress and anguish of heart and with many tears, not to grieve you but to let you know the depth of my love for you" (2 Cor. 2:4). Jesus wept. Are we, then, to be ashamed of our tears?

I used to think so. I hoped and fervently prayed that as I matured into a grown woman, I would gain increasing control over this embarrassing habit of crying at emotional moments. I would be tough in a tough world. I would grow up.

Daffo'ville Day changed my mind. We celebrate this seasonal holiday annually in the small village where I live on Cape Cod. Last year the mood was festive as the crowd gathered around the steps of our church to listen to the children's choir perform. My heart quickened, though, when I spotted our friend Joan.

Normally jovial and talkative, this morning Joan was silent, her face reddened with tears. A quick inquiry revealed her grief over the disappearance of their pet cat who had failed to return that morning. Childless, Joan's pets are her children. Our hopeful reassurances failed to cheer her.

Later, as I ferried my children to baseball games and birthday parties throughout the day, I kept seeing Joan's face. When her telephone went unanswered later that afternoon, my husband and I felt compelled to drive to their home some miles away. Joan and her husband were out in the yard as we drove in, but they did not look up. John was laying down a shovel, his face a mask of pain. Joan's face was in her hands and she was softly weeping. We joined hands and silently prayed over the simple grave.

A few days later, Joan approached us at church, gripped our hands and said simply, "Thanks. When you came to cry with me, I knew you really cared."

Not long afterwards I was present at another grave. At this funeral we buried Nancy, a dear friend who had just died of an inoperable brain tumor. There were hundreds of mourners this time, many of them one-time students of Nancy's Sunday school or Bible class. I joined a row of women alone, all of whom were softly weeping. Our tears, I thought, were our tribute. Joining in the family's grief was the most significant way in which we could minister to them.

As women, we minister to people in many ways. We teach the Bible and plan special events; we organize prayer chains and staff crisis pregnancy centers. But it is at its most elemental level that women's ministry is most powerful. It is women reaching out in the love of God—helping, supporting, teaching, and laughing with holy joy with those who laugh and weeping with those who grieve.

The women in Scripture were wives and mothers, judges and prophetesses, leaders of many, and followers of Christ. But the most powerful and poignant of women's ministry in Scripture included simple emotion—a woman gratefully washing Jesus' feet with her tears; a group of women in tears, watching as Jesus died on the cross; women, softly weeping, hurrying to be first at his tomb.

Another grave, another funeral. But women were there to offer holy tribute—a gift that the old saints would have called the "charism of tears."

In my forties I have learned at last not to despise my tears. They are a sign of my very humanity, my femininity. Most importantly, I am learning to offer my tears in ministry. I weep with God over the world and listen to his promptings as I reach out to his children—serving, loving, laughing, and yes, softly *weeping*.

Maggie Rowe says that at forty-plus, *"I am happy with most of the choices I have made in my life."* She has a degree in communications from Wheaton College and is active in a ministry of writing, drama, and conference speaking. Currently she serves as Women's Ministries Coordinator for the Evangelistic Association of New England. Maggie is the mother of Adam, Amber, and Jordan, and the wife of Michael Rowe, pastor of Osterville Baptist Church on Cape Cod.

Praise be to the God and
Father of our Lord Jesus
Christ, the Father of
compassion and the God
of all comfort, who comforts
us in all our troubles,
so that we can comfort
those in any trouble with
the comfort we ourselves
have received from God.
2 Corinthians 1:3-4

Growing Up
Jeanine K. Birdsall

English Teacher and Women's
Fellowship Coordinator
Saitama, Japan

Long-legged insects skittered among the reeds at the lake's edge where our little group had gathered. Still damp with dew, the clover bouquet from my daughter smelled sweet. The late July sun warmed our heads. The pastoral peace of our surroundings, at any other time, would have warmed my heart. But this morning was different.

Doug and I and our three children, along with a few close relatives, had come to this quiet park for the memorial service of our little son.

"While the child was still alive, . . ." Doug read from Scripture, his voice breaking and halting, "I thought, 'Who knows? The Lord may be gracious to me and let the child° live.' But now that he is dead, . . . I will go to him, but he will not return to me."

Then came the reading of Psalm 23. Dear and familiar words, yet that morning their comfort failed to reach the frozen abyss of my grief. Listening to them, I could only cry silently to God, *Oh, Lord! My little boy! The baby I'll never hold or kiss or sing to sleep. I miss his little presence within me so much. I know he is with you now. Please take good care of my little boy.*

The immense sorrow of losing a loved one is life's most devastating experience. Paradoxically, given into the hands of our loving heavenly Father, grief becomes one of the most powerful tools for shaping faith and character. Grief has been for me the quintessential mentor.

Though I have experienced lesser periods of loss and sadness, like the rejection of a friend or moving far from loved ones, my father's death and the loss of our baby last summer have been the deepest grief experiences of my life. Losing a child, one feels robbed of the future; losing a parent, one's past is taken.

My dad's death brought with it the loss of precious childhood security. I felt diminished by Dad's passing. I was lesser, our family was lesser and somehow shriveled. I missed his presence at the head of the table at family gatherings. I missed his hands, strong and work-roughened. I missed his voice in prayer. His voice always took on a special cadence when he prayed, and hearing that voice had, from earliest memory, made me feel that all was right with the world.

At the deepest level, I was forced to understand that life in this fallen world will have its sorrow. I had lived a life sheltered from sorrow. Now I had the little girl hands pried from my eyes and saw that God is not a Santa Claus-type who makes everything comfortable for people who follow him. Psalm 90 says as much: "You sweep men away in the sleep of death, . . . The length of our days is seventy years, . . . yet their span is but trouble and sorrow."

Put plainly, *I had to grow up.* And I did not like it. Nor did I like a God who would let my dad, a loving servant of his, die a lingering, painful death. During the days and weeks that followed my dad's death, when I tried to pray, I found myself crying out in great frustration and pain. "Who are you, God? I thought I knew you, but I can't understand a God who would allow such things to happen."

I felt no response, and sensed that no explanations would be forthcoming. I raged like a child who beats their fists against a parent, fighting for their own way. God let me beat on him with my angry, tearful prayers, all the while hugging me closer to him. Finally, after several months, I came to the end of myself. I stopped praying. I surrendered at last and was quiet.

In that quiet place, three ultimate and unshakable truths became clear. First, God is. Second, if God is, then he must be all the things he claims to be. Third, therefore God is good and can be trusted to redeem my suffering and use this experience for my good and his glory.

Dad's passing was a watershed in my life. Thereafter, I knew God and trusted his goodness. Losing our baby in the fifth month of pregnancy took me through another grief experience. With the news that there was no longer a heartbeat, something precious beyond calculation was ripped from me. Having dealt with death before, I knew already that the road to clean grief comes through surrender. Yet the pain was excruciating and the purifying fire was unbearable. Surrender was slow in coming and was full of anguish. I felt at times that I would perish through the process.

Ultimately, however, the results were the same. My grief, released to God, was redeemed. And I learned another great truth: *Surrender brings empowerment.* I am a different person now, stronger and able to assist others in similar circumstances.

Jeanie Birdsall delights in the fact that at forty-plus, *"I know who I am and feel glad anticipation for what I am becoming."* She is a graduate of Wheaton College and has a master's in intercultural studies from Fuller Theological Seminary. Jeanie stays busy as a missionary and wife to Douglas Birdsall, president of LIFE Ministries in Japan. She chairs the LIFE Member Care Task Force and is the mother of Stacia, Judson, and Jessamin.

Now Jesus wept. The Jews said, "Look how deeply He loved him!"
John 11:35-36, The Message

Life Without Maggie
Lynne M. Baab

Writer and Newsletter Editor
Seattle, Washington

It took me months to realize what I had lost. Experts talk about stages of grief. For me, the first stage was numbness. It lasted a long time.

Sure, I'd thought about death, particularly my parents' deaths. I'd prayed frequently that God would spare them prolonged illness. I grieved deeply when my grandmothers and great aunt died in the same year, when I was thirty-three. But this grief was different. After the numbness wore off, I felt as if a part of my life had been amputated. After all, Maggie had been my closest friend for a decade. She alone shared a wealth of memories of those years when our lives were intertwined. Now there's no one who understands that part of my life.

Maggie and I met the first week of college. It was freshman orientation, and we stood next to each other in line. We shared a background in the Episcopal Church (although I was rebelling against God that year).

We were both plump with long, dark blonde hair and wire-rimmed glasses. Often people in our dorm confused us for each other. I was slightly offended. After all, I was unique and didn't want to be mistaken for someone else. Maggie laughed.

I went to France for my sophomore year and there, because of a visit to a Christian community, I recommitted my life to Christ. I was concerned about returning to my home university because I knew my faith was fragile. I wrote to Maggie. Did she know a Christian woman with whom I could room? She wrote back and suggested that she and I live together.

Last week I came across a Christian bookmark Maggie sent me the summer before our junior year. In her unmistakable handwriting, she wrote a message on the back, calling me "roomie" and saying she was glad I was now truly her sister.

The last two years of college we were inseparable. We hosted small, intimate parties for close friends. We attended Christian conferences. We drove to the beach to fly kites and sing hymns into the wild wind.

And we talked. Countless hours of talking. We were endlessly fascinated with the complexity of people's personalities and the way they interacted. We always enjoyed analyzing where God fit into any picture. We looked to the future.

I had a job in Seattle after graduation, and she decided to venture along. We found a tiny, tacky apartment. For two years we continued our pleasant, intimate parties, this time in the form of omelette dinners with new friends. We continued to analyze the world, people, and the church in long, late-night conversations.

Then I met Dave, fell in love, and got married. All within months. Maggie got a job in North Carolina. Our paths crossed often in the following years, and we remained close friends. But Maggie married eight years after I did, and her children were much younger than mine, so our lives were out of sync. When she and her husband moved back to the Seattle area two years ago, I had just begun an intense job. I didn't have time to see her often.

She died at forty-one of a brain tumor, leaving behind her husband and two daughters, ages two and five. At first, during my numb stage, my tears were for her family. Two sweet girls growing up without their mother. I grieved that they would never know her energy and optimism, her gentle intelligence, and her remarkable ability to love. I grieved for her husband, so alone.

I know Maggie is dancing joyfully in the presence of the God she loved her whole life. But now, since the numbness has worn off, *I want her back*. I want her back to make up for the years we didn't see each other often. I want her back so we can share memories and discuss countless issues. I want her back to grow old together. I want her only a phone call away.

The world is not right without Maggie in it.

In this intense pain and loss, I have never sensed God saying, "Come on, snap out of it, have more faith." I have never perceived one moment of impatience on God's part with my grief and pain. I can only see Jesus, the man of sorrow, acquainted with grief, who stood at the tomb of *his* friend Lazarus and wept. He agrees that the world isn't right without Maggie and he stands beside me, whispering that he has conquered death as we weep together.

Lynne Baab believes the best part of being forty-plus is *"the wisdom of perspective."* A graduate of Fuller Theological Seminary, she plans and produces newsletters and mission materials for the Northwest/Alaska Presbyterian Synod. Lynn also does freelance writing and serves on the board of Opportunity International, a Christian development agency. Lynne is the mother of Jonathan and Michael and the wife of Dave Baab, a dentist.

*Praise be to the God and
Father of our Lord Jesus
Christ, the Father of
compassion and the God of all
comfort, who comforts us in
all our troubles, so that we
can comfort those in any
trouble with the comfort we
ourselves have received
from God.*
2 Corinthians 1:3-4

It's a Small World After All
Sarah Wetzel

Bible Teacher and Missionary
Cochabamba, Bolivia

"Señora Sara, please come with me to see Rosa's daughter. Her baby, Daisy, died last night!"

It was not the first time our camp caretaker's daughter, Sarita, had asked me to go with her to the nearby Quechua village. Her invitations sometimes put me in difficult situations. Like the time she asked me to take a "walk" with her, and she led me to the village church where an all-day meeting was in progress.

"Would you please sing a solo for us?" they asked. *Me, a solo? Me, who struggles in Spanish and knows about three words of Quechua? Me, dressed in all-American camp grubbies—blue jeans, sweatshirt, and baseball cap? Are they kidding?*

They were serious and probably thought I was rude when I declined.

Another time Sarita asked me to accompany her and a friend to her home. The friend was a new believer and Sarita wanted me to encourage her. It was a nice walk down the dirt roads to the other side of the town. But, in the end, I did not enjoy it because the lady asked me to be the "madrina" (financial godmother) of her little boy. I resented her request—I'd only just met her! I told myself that I was not going to walk with Sarita for a long time.

But this time Sarita's request was different. Rosa, the nearest neighbor to the camp, made bread for us when we lacked it. Her baby granddaughter, Daisy, had died in the night. I *wanted* to go and express my concern and friendship. Little did I know what blessing that afternoon would hold.

Sarita and I ducked into Rosa's windowless one-room home. On the table was the small white coffin. About a dozen people, all in black, huddled in heavy silence. The baby's mother and grandmother were outside preparing food for those coming to the wake. We sat there for what seemed like hours watching, listening, thinking, and praying.

Death is familiar in this village, especially the death of babies. Often babies are not named until after the first birthday because so many die before that time. But no matter how common, death stings. The young mother came in and wailed over the coffin—her sadness penetrated us all.

I knew what it was like to bury a baby—to have hopes and dreams die suddenly and senselessly. I, too, had wailed in grief at God when my first newborn had died.

Four men came in and bundled the coffin into an antique pick-up truck. We followed on foot to the cemetery, then stood in the chilly wind—waiting while the young men dug the tiny grave. When it was deep enough, the miniature coffin was lowered and the grave was filled and mounded. It was over.

Over for us, that is. We could go home to our loved ones, but Daisy's mother had to accept her empty arms and her broken heart. I hurt for her. Fourteen years after my own baby's burial, I still ache when I remember my own empty arms and heart.

But something changed in me that day. God taught a simple yet vital lesson to this idealistic young missionary. Before, when visiting the village, I saw only the *differences* and felt out of place and uncomfortable. That day at the burial, however, I saw that although our customs and language were quite diverse, our hearts were not. We *all* deeply need God to help us with this life, and the life to come. I repented of my self-centeredness and my lack of love for my Quechua neighbors. I asked God to help me truly love them and tell them about his love and salvation for all.

Sarah Wetzel is glad to be forty-plus because *"I'm closer to heaven!"* A graduate of Wheaton College, she serves with SIM International in Cochabamba, Bolivia, as a Bible teacher and is the mother of Johannah, Miah, Gabrielle, and Caris. Sarah and her husband, Jake Wetzel, have worked with many Christian camps and he is now the director of Camp Candelaria in the Andes mountains.

How great is the love the
Father has lavished on us, that
we should be called children of
God! And that is what we are!
1 John 3:1

Orphaned!
Janet Ellis Perez

Educator
Menlo Park, California

O*h, God, which one?* my mind prayed, as my friend Linda answered the phone in our hotel room. My body ached with fever and a sore throat, and my heart ached with the suspicion of impending tragedy. Far away in California, both of my parents had been sick, my dad was suffering from terminal cancer, and my mom had had a sudden stroke in that last week. I was teaching English in Beijing, China, and felt worlds away and helpless.

Linda slowly hung up the hotel phone. Her eyes avoided mine. I shouted, "Which one?"

"Your mom," she answered with her head down.

As the truth of my mother's death sank in, I felt numb and my legs were frozen and stiff as we made our way down the hallway to pay our room bill. How could I be living when one so precious to me had just stopped breathing? The ordinary but necessary steps of getting a taxi to the airport and getting on a plane seemed impossible and overwhelming.

We finally found an available flight. After thirteen fever-racked, brokenhearted hours, I arrived at my sister's house in the States. I fell into her arms and sobbed. Walking up the path to her front door, I could see flowers through the window: a huge arrangement on the piano, potted azaleas on the hearth, fresh plants and flowers everywhere. I hated them. The last chunk of my denial crumbled at the sight.

We buried my mom. A month later, my father died, joining Mother in the joy of being face to face with their Creator.

Reorienting my life around the fact of being an orphan at thirty-two was hard work. I was used to seeing myself and my decisions and life experiences in the context of being a daughter. Who was I now? Who would I be significant to now? I had no foothold to stand on. I felt that my teaching career in China, my finances, as well as a place to call home were all indefinite now.

In the weeks after my dad slipped away, I would pound out haltingly on the piano the hymn "Be Still, My Soul":

> Be still, my soul: the Lord is on thy side;
> Bear patiently the cross of grief or pain;
> Leave to thy God to order and provide;
> In every change He faithful will remain.
> Be still, my soul: thy best, thy heavenly Friend
> Thro' thorny ways leads to a joyful end.

As the words sank deep into my sorrowful heart, God himself rebuilt the foundation on which I stood. One by one, my fingers opened up to let go of my fears of being an orphan. What was true in the past wasn't true anymore. Galatians 4:6-7 says, "Because you are sons, God sent the Spirit of his Son into our hearts, the Spirit who calls out 'Abba, Father.'. . . Since you are a son [or daughter], God has made you also an heir." Slowly the comforting sense of being adopted into God's family permeated my life and brought great comfort.

Marriage became a miraculous reality, and swiftly afterwards came a daughter and then a son. The meaning of being God's daughter really hit home to me as I experienced parenting myself. I asked the Lord, "Now what? How do I parent?"

Recently there was a mound of bills and correspondence accumulating on my desk. It took me days to get through it. Kristy and Steven would play contentedly nearby for a while. Then the bickering would start. Irritated, I'd separate them or put down my pen to find something to keep them occupied. After a few weeks of this, I read about how God longs for us to meet him with our whole hearts. He's very present with us, not just doing his thing while I do mine.

The picture of my focusing on paying bills with my children playing on their own around my feet flooded into my mind. And I remembered the busyness of my own parents as well. As wonderful as they were, some difficulties in my parents' marriage kept them from having a full emotional platter to offer me as I was growing up. Typical of the fruit of families involved in some dysfunction, I not only was repeating that habit of emotional distance with my children, but I was projecting it onto my image of God, too. I assumed he cared as my Father, but that he was really too preoccupied to get involved in my life.

I recalled Galatians 4:6. God had given me his Spirit who calls out, "Abba, Father." God is not like my parents, or like me as I parent my children. He has not left me orphaned. He has adopted me, taking full responsibility for my life as his heir.

My time with my kids is now more purposeful and frequent. And so is my time with my heavenly Father, who is with me in his fullness, nurturing and guiding. He is filling the void left in my heart those years ago, and is replacing it with the reality of his perfect parenting.

Janet Perez, almost forty, graduated from Columbia Bible College and also has a master's in special education. She serves as a small group leader in her church and works for the Foundation for Advanced Christian Training, a missions organization. Janet is the mother of Kristy and Steven, and the wife of Ken Perez, a financial analyst.

Jesus said to them,
"You're blessed when
you feel you've lost
what is most dear to you.
Only then can you be
embraced by the One
most dear to you."
Matthew 5:4, The Message

Enjoy God Forever

Sandra L. Hackett

Minister, Writer, and Small Group
Consultant
Bellevue, Washington

It was one of a series of messages on the answering machine that afternoon: "Sandy, this is Dr. Woods. Please call me when you get in."

Five months into a difficult third pregnancy, I had talked to him often. However, I wasn't expecting a call back that day, and the results of my amniocentesis weren't due for another ten days.

I phoned the office. "Mrs. Hackett, he's with another patient. Just a minute and I'll get him." My throat tightened. Doctors don't usually take calls when they're seeing patients.

"Mrs. Hackett, thanks for calling back. I have some news. We have heard from the laboratory, and you're going to have a little boy."

That was good news! Our two daughters were eager for a boy, "to keep dad company in the locker room when we go swimming." I waited for the doctor to congratulate me, to say those words I was so certain of—that everything else looked great. . . . I waited, and then heard instead, "Your son has Down Syndrome. I'm very sorry."

The next minutes, hours, and days blurred with grief. I called my husband, Dave, and together we began a round of seeing my doctor, visiting schools, and interviewing therapists. While offering us real hope for all our son's life could be, they also painted worst-case scenarios, and asked us to decide if we could live with that.

Gathering all the information we could in those first intense days, Dave and I retreated to our favorite beach, huddling in the tiny camper over his parent's Datsun pickup. We walked the beach, threw rocks at the waves, and found it too painful to talk. We wrote alone in our journals, then read what the other had written as we tried to share the sadness that threatened to undo us.

I was new to this kind of fear and grief. My faith had been founded during my childhood, and built during years when the circumstances of my life turned out better than I could have hoped. Nurturing churches, remarkable family and friends, a solid theological education, outstanding mentors—I was grateful for a strong context in which to establish my faith. Now, what I knew and had proclaimed to be true was tested, and I had to act on it as truth. "What is the chief end of man?" the Westminster Catechism asks. "The chief end of man is to glorify God, and enjoy him forever."

The chief end of any of our lives is our relationship with God. We were created to enjoy him, not primarily to serve him or to accomplish great things for him. God created us simply to be in his presence, to delight in his character and company.

This baby boy I was carrying could do that. My greatest hope for each of our children is that they would come to know the love of Christ, and to love him in return. That was my prayer for our daughters, and it became my prayer for this new little boy we named Peter Glenn.

It became an urgent prayer for him during an endless ultrasound while the technologist named for us every abnormality she was looking for. And when my husband lost his job in a staffing redesign, we learned to pray that we might know Christ and remain confident in his care for us, no matter how severely circumstances shake us.

The final blow came just a few short weeks before Peter's due date. Feeling no movement, I went first to the doctor and then to the radiologist. No heartbeat and no fetal activity. Entangled in the umbilical cord, Peter had died.

I was home from the hospital, curled up in bed, when my five-year-old, Anna, came to talk. She crawled under the covers with me and said, "Mom, is Peter okay in heaven without his mommy to take care of him?"

Tears. "Yes, Anna, he is. We're the ones who are sad. Jesus is taking good care of Peter."

Silence. "But does Jesus let Peter snuggle in bed with him?" "Yes, Anna, I think he does."

Sandy Hackett believes that this age brings a *"discovery of myself in the midst of the deep pain of the last years."* She holds degrees from Seattle Pacific University and Fuller Theological Seminary. An ordained Presbyterian minister, Sandy enjoys teaching Bible and encouraging churches in small group ministry. She is the mother of Anna and Katelyn and the wife of David Hackett, a Presbyterian pastor and missionary.

*And he took the children in
his arms, put his hands on
them and blessed them.
Mark 10:14-16*

My Father's
Arms

Dorothea M. S. Glatte

Insurance Administrator
Hartford, Connecticut

I'll never forget a nightmare I had as a child. Hot flames
shot out of shattered stained glass windows, licking at the
stone masonry and slate roof of the gothic cathedral. I was
trapped. Suddenly I woke up, my heart relentlessly pounding against my chest. I grabbed my comforter, slid back-
wards out of my child-size bed, and ran towards my
parents' bedroom.

Terribly frightened, I faced a seemingly endless trek
through the darkened kitchen, dining room, and living
room, until I could reach the safety of my parents' arms.
My comforter slowed progress considerably, but it shielded
me against monsters in the dark.

As I rounded the corner into the living room, I stopped
dead in my tracks. There, near my folks' bedroom door,
loomed a hunched figure by the wing-tipped armchair.
Fiery images quickly faded in comparison to the new threat
hindering my path to security. I froze in fear. Then I heard
whispers coming from the depths of the chair.

"*Gib uns unser tägliches Brot.*" ("Give us this day our daily bread.") The voice sounded familiar. I crept forward holding my comforter. "*Und führe uns nicht in Versuchung.*" ("And lead us not into temptation.")

"Papa!" I called. The kneeling figure rose and lifted me—comforter and all—into his strong arms.

I will never forget my relief in discovering my papa in the darkness of that room. He held me in his arms, sat down, and asked, "What's the matter, little one?"

"I had a bad dream about fire, Papa," I said. "I'm scared."

"You don't need to be afraid, Dorothea. Our loving Lord Jesus is always with us. He wants to help us get rid of scary feelings," Papa responded. "Let's talk with Jesus about this and then I'll tuck you back into bed."

The blessing of my father's living example of his walk with the Lord Jesus graced the initial twenty-seven years of my life. Each day, without fail, Papa rose at 5:00 A.M. to pray. This was an essential, life-transforming part of my childhood experience. I later discovered that Jesus practiced this discipline of morning prayer (Mark 1:35).

Papa prayed about the minutest details of our family's daily needs, as well as those found in the workplace and the world. He did not hesitate to share his deepest feelings with his heavenly Father. Papa taught me to be honest with the Lord—always telling him everything, whether good, bad, or indifferent.

My father wasn't always right in his views or judgment, but he sincerely desired to walk with Jesus. Papa struggled with a natural tendency to quickly lose his temper. Yet he wasn't too proud to acknowledge his failures and ask for forgiveness from those he offended. It was a painful reminder that he was a sinner, saved by God's grace.

Papa instilled within me a deep love of the Old and New Testaments. He led our family in daily devotions. We would alternately read the designated Bible verses and then talk about how to apply them in our daily experiences. Papa insisted that my brothers and I memorize a weekly Bible verse by learning it with us and corporately reciting it at each meal.

My father talked about Jesus when he rose, when he sat at the dinner table, when he walked along the city streets, and when he lay down at night. Papa brought Deuteronomy 6:4-9 to life. His desire to know the Lord inspired him to read extensively and attend Christian conferences.

I often sparred with Papa about biblical interpretation. Sometimes the debate was very intense and I would say, "I love you, Papa, even though I don't agree with your theological interpretation of this passage." But these debates laid a strong foundation which enabled me to face occasional faith challenges later.

My papa died in 1981. There isn't a single day that goes by that I don't miss his kneeling silhouette, protective arms, and praying hands. Papa taught me to love, to walk with, and to rely upon my Lord and Savior, Jesus Christ.

I know that the Lord will rescue me from every evil and, ultimately, he will bring me safely into his presence (2 Tim. 4:18). Then I'll be able to see him face to face and praise him, along with my papa and all of the saints forever and ever!

Dorothea Glatte believes that the best part about being forty-plus is *"looking back and seeing God's faithfulness throughout my life."* She is a graduate of Trinity College and Gordon-Conwell Theological Seminary. In addition to her duties as a compliance administrator at Aetna Life Insurance Company, Dorothea is a Bible teacher and lay minister and currently serves on the Grace Lutheran Church Council.

V. INVESTING IN THE FUTURE

Someone once told me, "Our children are the gift we give to a world we will never see." Just yesterday I read a greeting card that said, "We all should plant a few trees we will never sit under." Quite a mandate for motherhood, I'd say! One friend describes her occupation as "Investor in Futures"—and she doesn't mean the stock market.

I can't help but wonder how many young women today would say they want to be mothers when they grow up. It seems motherhood has gotten a pretty bad rap lately, and I'm not sure why. Mothers have the ability to set the whole tone of the home, and therefore, the future. And frankly, it's the hardest professional job I've ever had.

When Mother Teresa won the Nobel Peace Prize, someone asked her, "What can we do to promote world peace?"

Her response? "Go home and love your family."

This past Mother's Day I was asked to speak on the subject of motherhood. I chose the title "When Mama Ain't

Happy, Ain't Nobody Happy!" which is one of my favorite southern phrases, and a truth I strongly believe.

I told those attending some of what I've learned along the way. We moms need *soul care* as my friend, Adele, would say. If we can't find meaning and worth in God's unconditional love and marvelous promises, then how can we pass anything of value on to the next generation? And, if it's not passed on, well, let's just say there won't be a whole lot of trees left to sit under.

By the time I finally became a mother, in my thirties, I was ready (or so I thought). After all, I'd read all the appropriate books, observed my friends making parenting mistakes, and had enough outside-the-home achievement to give me the confidence to decide to stay home.

I was singularly blessed to have the privilege of adopting three children, ages nine, seven, and four. However, walking out of court with their newly revised birth certificates, I felt like someone who had just stopped by the church nursery and taken home three children (any three children). Now I had to get to know them, discover their personalities, strengths, fears, and what they needed most from me. Needless to say, it was daunting.

I loved them to pieces. I also made quite a few mistakes.

But my God is a God of grace and my children have proven amazingly resilient. Five years later, I gave birth to our fourth child and entered another high learning curve— infancy through preschool. It seems I have spent years trying to get this motherhood thing right!

Recently a sports reporter interviewed my now twenty-year-old son, Justin, about his place on the United States Tennis Team for the Special Olympics World Games. As I watched their interchange, I was amazed at Justin's poised and well-thought-out answers to the reporter's questions.

So what if he can only read at a first- or second-grade level, he sure can talk!

I was a little taken aback when the reporter asked me, "Was it hard when Justin was growing up?"

Was it hard? My thoughts returned to the early days when Justin was so frustrated, so hyperactive, so competitive, so needy. "Yes, it was hard," I admitted. "But his father and I believed then, as we do now, that *all* children need the same things—unconditional love, encouragement, challenge, and accountability. It's just that children with special challenges such as Justin's need everything with an extra dose of patience, love, and grace."

I am an investor in futures. When I take the time to read stories, pray with my children before school, cheer at tennis matches, wash clothes, send care packages to college, help with scouts, sew on badges, mend a doll's broken arm, sit through hours of dance rehearsal, fill out financial aid applications, go to endless special education forums, and drive all over town, I am saying to them, "You are important to me and I will go the extra mile to help you feel secure, worthy, and loved."

When we mamas look to our husbands, our kids, our things, our titles, our jobs, or anything else to bring us happiness, we will come away frustrated, bitter, and disillusioned. God alone, through the power of the Holy Spirit, is the One who gives us strength, wisdom, humor, fortitude, and yes, even happiness, to plant our little acorns and nurture them into mighty trees.

The women you will meet in the last section of this book realize the importance of emptying themselves so that others might be filled. I'm sure they would all agree that, while mothering doesn't bring too many public accolades, it certainly brings a sense of personal purpose and satisfaction.

We don't need to worry about the future—that's not our job. Our job is to invest in the short time we have with our children *now,* and leave the rest to God.

*"For I know the plans I have
for you," declares the Lord,
"plans to prosper you and not
to harm you, plans to give
you hope and a future."*
Jeremiah 29:11

A Divine Interruption
Sharol Rhodes Hayner

Composer and Worship Leader
Madison, Wisconsin

"Do you want to be pregnant?" the nurse asked while
she scribbled on my chart.

"Well . . . I don't know," I stammered. On my third
course of antibiotics, I couldn't account for the continued
fatigue and interrupted rhythms in my body. So here I was
taking, of all things, a pregnancy test. At forty-two, I
thought the nurse should be asking about premenopausal
symptoms.

"There's no doubt," replied the nurse, "you're pregnant."

How can this be? I thought, the world whirling around
me. *I have a ten-year-old and a twelve-year-old. I'm just discovering what I am about. I'm beginning to have the freedom to
travel with my husband, to make decisions about my future.*

As I burst into tears, she quickly responded, "Of
course, you could do something about it." But no, I would
never do anything to this baby.

As I drove home, I wrestled with God. How could this be a gift—this grand interruption, this unexpected and unwanted "blessing"? All around me, friends were struggling with infertility. Why, God, was I pregnant and not them? And what if something turned out to be wrong with this baby or I lost him or her? Already, the hope of new life had captured me and the fears began to set in.

It was Advent, the preparation for the coming of Jesus, and during those four weeks before Christmas, I lived and breathed with Mary, the young maid who also asked, "How can this be?" The sermon series at our church, "Tidings of Glory," led me into deep struggles with the truths of the familiar Christmas story. No one—not Joseph or Mary or the shepherds—ever expected to have life interrupted by God. Each was simply going about the business of daily living. Then, life-changing, dream-shattering news—which the angels announced as good news of great joy.

Each person met the bearer of this good news with fear. It was frightening to be interrupted by an angel. It didn't sound like good news at first. Where was the joy? Joy came to Mary and Joseph only after *they chose to believe the words of the angel and pursue the way of God.*

Joy came to the shepherds after they left their sheep and, like crazy men, returned to Bethlehem to find this baby announced by the angels. God didn't ask Mary, Joseph, or the shepherds to do the impossible, but he did ask them to do the improbable. And God asked that each one would take the next step of obedience, believing that the news of the angels was good, true, and hopeful.

I realized that God asked the same of me. My life journey wasn't laid out, but the next steps were clear. I was being asked to choose to believe that the plans of God for me were good, giving me and our family a hope and a future. I had to trust a gracious God with this pregnancy and believe that somehow this baby was a part of God's plan.

And God's plan has been good. Drew has come to us as a special gift of God's grace and love. We didn't know how much we needed him. He has united our family in ways we could never have accomplished on our own. He has brought laughter to every meal and joy to countless family members and friends who participate in his antics and nurture. Surprisingly, God has also provided opportunities for me to do and become what I never dreamed possible. Life didn't shut down with a new baby; it simply turned an unexpected corner.

Of course, there have been challenges. Each one of us has had to flex. God has dramatically highlighted my selfishness and my reluctance to give up my dreams to discover God's new thing. And sometimes, when my husband and I ponder the future, we can't imagine having two in college and a first-grader.

Am I now better able to receive God's interruptions in my life? Sometimes. But most often I respond with that same fearful, "How can this be?" I cling to the familiar and the safe. Knowing, however, that God's ways are often different from mine, and believing that they are meant to prosper and not harm me, my daily prayer has become, "Lord, give me eyes to see you, ears to hear your voice, and courage to take the next step toward you." For you see, when you least expect it, God seems to show up.

Sharol Hayner is glad at forty-plus to *"have a bit more patience and a greater sense of who God has made me and what he is calling me to."* She is a graduate of Wellesley College and earned a master's in music from the University of Massachusetts. Sharol stays quite busy with ministry opportunities as the wife of Stephen Hayner, president of InterVarsity Christian Fellowship. She is the mother of Emilie, Chip, and Drew.

For the Lord delights
in you.
Isaiah 62:4

Maybe God Laughs

Robin Jones Gunn

Author
Portland, Oregon

My five-year-old son didn't know I was watching him, listening from the upstairs window. He and his little friend, Asenath, had been playing in the backyard sandbox for over an hour, and were now taking a break, swinging together in the hammock.

"What do you want to do now?" Ross asked Asenath.

"I dunno. What do you want to do?"

"You want to climb the apple tree?"

"No."

"I know!" Ross said. "Let's play Adam and Eve!"

I leaned closer to the window to get a full view and thought, *If either of them start taking their clothes off . . .*

But Asenath had already squelched the idea. "No, I don't want to play Adam and Eve," she said, shaking her golden locks.

"Ah, come on!" Ross coaxed. "It'll be fun! I'll be Adam and you can be Eve."

"I don't want to be Eve," Asenath said, folding her arms defiantly.

"You can't be Adam," Ross reasoned. "I'm the boy and you're the girl. You have to be Eve."

"I don't want to be Eve," Asenath said slowly, "I want to be . . . God!"

Ross looked at her in surprise. "Hey!" he said brightly, his expression reflecting his sudden insight. "That's just what the snake said! You can be the snake!"

I ran into the hallway so the young theologians wouldn't hear my roaring laughter. Where does my son come up with this stuff?

He's eleven now. A "tweener." Caught somewhere between being a kid and a young adult. I saw this quite clearly when we were at the lake a few months ago. I heard some girls giggling and from my beach chair perch, I scanned the water until I saw three junior high girls splashing water at a boy and then running away, giggling as he sprayed them back.

Ahh, youth! I thought, remembering my wonder years when my girlfriends and I learned everything we needed to know about flirting by teasing boys. *I was just like those skinny little girls relentlessly chasing boys!*

Suddenly my opinion of those giggling girls came to a shrieking halt. Those girls weren't flirting with boys. They were chasing *my* boy! My only son, who was obviously far too young to respond to these, these . . . hussies!

But he was responding! He was splashing them back and smiling and looking awfully manly with his chest all puffed out and his hands on his hips, defying those girls to ever try splashing him again! He was turning into a young man right in front of my eyes, and I wasn't sure how I felt.

Later that afternoon, all my fears dissolved with the mere plunk of a stranger's quarter. We stopped at the grocery store. My man-child pushed a cart from the parking lot to the front of the store, chasing his little sister the whole way and torturing her with threats that he was going to run her over. They reached the entrance of the store before I did and stood together, watching a sweet grandma lift her toddler onto one of the three horses on the coin-operated merry-go-round. The dear woman turned to my daughter and asked, "Would you like to ride, too?"

Rachel charged for the painted steed and right on her heels came my "tweener." Old enough to flirt with girls yet young enough to still want to hop on the kiddie ride. It didn't matter to him that his legs were too long to fit under the handles sticking out of the horse's head. His right leg dragged on the ground and he had to duck his head under the twirling canopy.

I laughed silently while the quarter ride took him around one last time. I knew next time he was offered such a ride he'd probably realize it wasn't cool and hang back. And the next time the girls splashed at the lake he might even do more than just splash back. He might actually talk to them. So, I watched with a bittersweet chuckle caught in my throat.

I had that same feeling last week while I was praying about something very important to me. Only the bitter-sweet chuckle wasn't caught in my throat, but rather in God's throat, or so it seemed. I somehow got the idea that maybe as God watched me pray, he was lovingly swallowing a chuckle. My prayer was rather grandiose for a "tweener" Christian.

I prayed with my hands on my hips, chest puffed out, daring God to answer me. Then only moments later, I ducked my head on this spinning merry-go-round of faith, feeling his eyes on me as I kept trying all the things that used to fit in my spiritual life. Only I've outgrown them and my leg hangs over the side and drags me down.

Woe is me, for I am a "tweener"! Suspended between spiritual and mortal, heaven and earth. So sure of my faith and so timid at the same time. I prayed my grandiose prayer and then feared God might be disappointed in me, disgusted with my immaturity.

But then I thought of my son. I am far from being a perfect parent and yet I know how to give good gifts to my children. I didn't correct his theology that afternoon in the backyard with Asenath. And I certainly didn't embarrass him in front of the girls at the lake or tell him to get off the kiddie ride. Instead, I watched him grow and I laughed, delighted in him simply because he is my son.

In this I am greatly comforted. Because perhaps through all the stages of my growing faith and in the midst of all my bumbling, maybe my heavenly Father is not disgusted or disappointed with me after all. Maybe like a loving parent, he watches me grow and delights in me simply because I am his daughter. And maybe, just maybe, sometimes I make him laugh.

Robin Gunn, at forty-plus, is *"looking back and feeling content with what God has accomplished so far in my life—makes me eager and curious to see what he still has up his sleeve."* She is a graduate of Biola University and the author of twenty-six books, including the Christy Miller series of teen fiction and the recent novel, *Secrets.* A former radio broadcaster, Robin speaks frequently at schools and conferences. She is the mother of Ross and Rachel and the wife of Ross Gunn, a youth minister currently finishing his master's in counseling.

*No eye has seen, no ear
has heard, no mind has
conceived what God
has prepared for those
who love him.*
1 Corinthians 2:9

Promises Fulfilled
Judith Weber Smathers

Women's Discipleship
Arlington, Virginia

Ever since I was sixteen years old I had wanted to be married and have a family! I clung to the above words of 1 Corinthians 2:9, and to John 16:24, "Until now you have not asked for anything in my name. Ask and you will receive, and your joy will be complete." These became God's special promises for my life.

But at age forty, it looked as if those dreams were to die. I must admit that they died a very slow, painful death. For many years I had tried to stand on God's Word and not focus on my circumstances. I had also done everything humanly possible to correct the perceived horrible single state of my life.

At the same time I struggled, begged, cajoled, pleaded, demanded, and asked God to help me, but nothing visible happened. Finally, I gave up on both marriage and children and said, "If you want something to happen in these areas, you do it. I give up!"

At that point I began to make the most of my life as a single adult. Surprisingly, at that point things began to happen. God brought a man into my life whom I had known fifteen years before, who had also never married. This man was to my mind the *most* unlikely potential spouse in the whole world. When we had first met, I considered him very sophisticated and probably only interested in others of like tastes.

But as we got to know each other again, I could see that we had both changed. God had brought two people who were very different before to a very similar place fifteen years later. Two and a half years after we met again, and sustained by many interventions of God, John and I were married.

God's wonderful promises had become a living reality!

So much for being married. The next snag was the issue of children. Immediately before our engagement, I was told I had gone through early menopause. What a devastating blow to my deep and longing desire to have a family. However, seeing God's prior answer to my prayer for a husband so gloriously fulfilled, I thought the baby situation would probably right itself after we were married and settled. Again, as my life verses instructed, I asked God for this so that my joy might be made complete. The fact that my great-aunt had her first and only child at age forty-six was also an inspiration.

After a year of marriage we had no children. We did our part and began some fertility procedures which proved fruitless. John was quite clear that he didn't feel he could adopt. Again, on my knees, I told God I couldn't do anything, but if he wanted us to have children, he would have to change John's mind.

And he did! John can tell you the exact moment when a desire to embrace a baby through adoption dropped into his heart.

Now, where would we find the children to adopt? Many people said that this would be impossible because of the shortage of adoptable children and our advanced ages. But what God begins, he completes.

Through the prayers of faithful friends and a network of believers, we beat the impossible odds and adopted our first child, a girl, in March 1988 and our second child, a boy, in December 1989. Both were given up for adoption by two young women, who had been brought back to a vital relationship with Jesus Christ through their birth experiences. Our children are more wonderful than I ever could have hoped or conceived—literally! Through our agony, God's Word had once again proven true.

The fulfillment of my heart's desires has not only filled out my life, but has also limited it in some ways. Mothering little ones has been the hardest and yet the most satisfying thing I have ever done. It has taught me how many strokes I had received in the past from serving Christ in an open and visible way, trying to please others more than Christ. For those of us whose vocation is primarily at home, having our labor seen and acknowledged is rare. Our focus instead is to please him who sees everything—even our thoughts.

My first forty years taught me the futility of trying to bring about God's will on my own. Now my motherhood prayer each day is to glorify the Lord in all things, whether that be driving a car pool or cleaning the family room for the fifth time that day. After being up all night with a sick child, a forty-plus body does not bounce back as quickly as a twenty-plus one does! Through the demands of mothering and being a wife, I have learned to an ever-deepening degree that the Lord must become our strength.

Marriage has also brought a flesh-and-blood husband to deal with. God often works through my husband in wonderful ways to provide, encourage, support, and love. But where the Lord has no limitations, my wonderful husband does. Of necessity, I have also learned here that prayer is a great gift in marriage to enable both partners to become more like Christ individually and corporately.

The Bible says that "the preparations of the heart are of the Lord." Having been single for many years, I now have many opportunities to meet with older singles and encourage them to seek Christ in these years. What a great joy! Many of their waitings have been fulfilled also. Also, based on our perseverance of faith, John and I have had the great privilege to be divinely instrumental in several of our friends' adoption searches. How true that the Lord gives us comfort in order that we may comfort others.

Finally, being married with young children has opened up myriad opportunities to meet with women and their young children. We are finding that our respective strengths and weaknesses are meshed together in a most wonderful way.

In retrospect, I see now how God's transformation of my life in so many areas during my twenties and thirties had truly prepared me for my season of midlife. Once a person has truly tasted life with Christ, nothing else satisfies!

> **Judy Smathers** is thankful to have *"had forty-plus wonderful years to learn about God's faithfulness."* She holds degrees from Penn State University and the Young Life Institute of Biblical Studies. In addition to mothering Townley and John-Samuel, Judy helps organize small groups and retreats for women. She is married to John Smathers.

But if anyone obeys his word,
God's love is truly made
complete in him. This is how
we know we are in him:
Whoever claims to live in him
must walk as Jesus did.
1 John 2:5-6

A Legacy of Faith

Janice P. Howard

Bible Study Leader
Lindenhurst, Illinois

"Our obedience to God matters," the speaker said. "It takes some of the twistedness out of life for others." I sat there, a newlywed, twentysomething young woman, captivated by this vibrant, godly, middle-aged woman who was giving the talk at our church's mother-daughter banquet. And I knew she and her husband believed this truth because of the way I saw them faithfully live it out.

In their various leadership capacities within our church, as well as the large parachurch organization with which they served, I watched them manage assets wisely and resourcefully. To have any dealings with them was to be treated with utmost integrity. They could laugh heartily and welcome a wide range of people hospitably. When they sang, it was with gusto! To be with them was to sense a joy of life, wonder, anticipation, and discovery.

It seemed to me that each of them carried deep within a sense of God's call upon their life and each held a deep-seated commitment to obedience to God. How faithfully they engaged students' questions with articulate and well-reasoned answers based on biblical truth. In her writings, she inspired us to see God at work in all of life and to live our lives according to those implications.

In the various Bible study guides she has authored, one can see her keen and searching mind. She consistently expected us to approach the Word with three questions: What does it say? What does it mean? What does it mean to me? Inherent in all this was the belief that the Bible holds authority for our lives and thus, we each needed to wrestle with the question of what obedience to this truth would mean for our lives.

Obedience to God matters. That thought arrested my attention in a powerful way that evening and continues to this day. It reinforces all that I've been raised to believe and practice in my family, and it resonates because of the authenticity of the speaker's lifestyle which I had been privileged to observe. The words of an old treasured hymn we sang often in the little rural church of my childhood echoes the importance of obeying God:

> I would be true, for there are those who trust me;
> I would be pure, for there are those who care;
> I would be strong, for there is much to suffer;
> I would be brave, for there is much to dare.

The other day as I counseled with a young seminary wife, it occurred to me that much of what I said to her were truths that had been deeply imprinted in me by this much-admired older couple. Indeed, they had served as divinely inspired, spiritual mentors at a very strategic point in my life. Now, in my forties, and by God's orchestration, I find myself in a similar place in the lives of others of his appointment. I am humbled by what a sacred trust that is and by how much my obedience matters.

Yes, I want to keep the faith, partly in tribute to such fine and faithful mentors. But I also want to invest in the future. I want to be found faithful by those who will follow me: not only my own two precious daughters and their friends, but also by many seminary student wives who will pass on to still other women what they saw modeled for them at a strategic point in their lives. It is a calling worthy of my commitment far past the age of forty.

So, I *would* be true, for there are those who trust me, and who have been entrusted to me. I deem that a very sacred trust indeed.

Jan Howard is glad at forty-plus for *"some life experiences which lend wisdom and stability in my day-to-day decisions and responsibilities."* She has degrees from Ohio State University and the Wheaton Graduate School. Jan is a mentor for seminary student wives, is on staff with the Neighborhood Bible Study organization, and also does some conference speaking. She is the mother of Christina and Melody and the wife of David Howard, Jr., professor at Trinity Evangelical Divinity School.

And whoever welcomes
a little child like this
in my name welcomes me.
Matthew 18:5

My First-Born Son

Susan McDonald Wood

School Principal
Sevierville, Tennessee

In his most loving, fatherly tone, my doctor leaned down and said, "Your baby has an anomaly. Have you heard of spina bifida?"

These words came after twelve hours of intense labor followed by an emergency C-section. I was fully awake because I had elected an epidural. After months spent preparing for natural childbirth and the hours of pain doing my breathing, I wanted to be alert for my baby's arrival.

Despite the anxiety of being sped around the hospital on a gurney for tests to determine why the baby wasn't ready to be delivered, I tried to focus on the inevitable moment of joy when all of my fears would subside and my beautiful, healthy baby would be placed in my arms. I had been delighted to hear the doctor say, "It's a boy!" But instead of receiving him into my waiting arms, I heard quiet, serious conversation among the medical staff. That's when my doctor came to speak to me.

"No, I haven't heard of spina bifida. What is it? Can I see my baby?" I responded weakly.

"I'm sorry. We'll have to take him to the special care nursery for evaluation," he insisted.

I was taken to the recovery room. Alone and numb, I listened to the cries and whimpering of mothers and their newborns around me. I had hoped to be on the phone, speaking to grandparents and aunts and uncles experiencing the joy of their new roles. I expected to be taking photos of the most beautiful baby ever born. Instead, I didn't even know if my baby was alive or what other agonizing future we might be facing.

Dear Lord, you haven't lost track of me, have you? I can't imagine anything more miserable than being in a sterile room full of germicidal smells and the ugly moans and bitter complaints of women in pain from physical childbirth. Here I am fearing the loss of my most basic dream—motherhood—and I can't even cry. Lord, give me something to hope for.

I felt the sensation of God's warmth and presence powerfully in the moments that followed that prayer. God knew how to meet me, just as he had the day I trusted him for salvation and the weight of my sin was lifted. Now, I heard again that still, small voice comforting me with gentle correction: "Did you really mean it when you gave your life to me? Did you count the cost? Have you planned this child's life or is that something you had already entrusted to me? I didn't want him to play professional football or to become a lawyer. I have other plans for him, special plans. All that matters is what his life will mean years from now and only I can plan that perfectly. I have answered your prayers to work out my will for your life and his. Can anything be better than that?"

When my husband and the doctor finally came with a report four hours later, not even the news that my son was severely brain-damaged could dispel the peace which God had given to me. I knew "the peace of God which passes understanding" and "which guards my heart and mind" in a way not otherwise possible. The path of my life changed that day in 1978 while I was still only twenty-two.

As I enter my fortieth year, that baby boy is now sixteen and driving with hand controls. I would not trade him or the past sixteen years of my life for anything! I couldn't have imagined what the life God had planned for me would be, but I can say with complete sincerity, "Our God is an awesome God!"

Paul, named for the apostle because of his thorn in the flesh, is a beautiful Christian. He is far more wonderful than all of my anticipated hopes and dreams. Although he has had twenty surgeries and innumerable procedures, he has provided tremendous inspiration to his younger brothers and has repeatedly defied his medical prognosis.

We believe that God has answered prayer on his behalf and have had many opportunities to attest to this. Many people have come to Christ during crisis periods of Paul's life. He has been reading since he was four and is already committed to a life of ministry. His favorite Scripture is one that he can say firsthand with the apostle Paul, "When I am weak, then I am strong" (2 Cor. 12:10).

Susan Wood rejoices that at forty-plus she *"has a fully developed identity and a clear sense of calling."* She is a graduate of Mississippi State University and is the principal of St. Andrew's School and co-founder of Wears Valley Ranch, a youth home. Susan is the mother of Paul, Clayton, and Andrew and the wife of James Wood, pastor-at-large of Mt. Vernon Baptist Church and executive director of Wears Valley Ranch.

Anyone who loves his father
or mother more than me is
not worthy of me; anyone who
loves his son or daughter more
than me is not worthy of me;
and anyone who does not
take his cross and follow me
is not worthy of me.
Matthew 10:37-38

Learning
to Let Go
Mary Wilken

Writer and Bible Teacher
Asheville, North Carolina

Early in my faith journey I learned the importance of relinquishment. I lived in an old house with six other students close to the University of Minnesota East Campus. The atmosphere typified college life in the early 1970s—parties, books, constant commotion, and a mural of "Mr. Natural" painted on the living room wall.

But then something remarkable happened to my boyfriend. Terry went home for the summer to work and save money. There two of his high school friends confronted him with the claims of Christ. Five hours later, Terry knelt beside his bed in a prayer of surrender. His dramatically changed life convinced me his faith was real. A few days later, I too became a Christian.

Since we naively thought we two were the only Christians on the university campus, I thought our relationship was critical to my survival. We still attended parties with our friends. But while they rolled joints to the blasting sounds of music, we talked to them about the peace Christ had given us.

Our shared faith drew us even closer, but I began to have an unwanted, persistent thought—I knew I had to let go of this important friendship. If I wanted my faith to be authentic, I had to be willing to go it alone with Jesus. The thought terrified me.

I refused it for several agonizing weeks till I finally gave in, knowing it was the only way to preserve my newly found peace. Awkwardly I proclaimed my intentions: "Jesus, I don't understand this at all, and I'm scared. But I choose to trust you. I'm willing for it to be just you and me. Please help me."

Within a week, Terry proposed to me.

We've been married twenty-two years now. Granted, not all relinquishment produces such expedient results! But the *outcome* of letting go belongs to God. The purpose is to put him first in our lives by entrusting all we have to him. My first experience in letting go proved to be a significant lesson and only the beginning of learning to trust God in relationships.

My prenuptial relinquishment of Terry was just the first of many times I've had to let go of him. After several years of marriage, I came to the conclusion that it was *Jesus*, not my husband, who could and would meet my emotional needs. I frequently need reminding of that. And relinquishment actually gives me great freedom in relating to Terry. When I am not demanding, he is much more willing to be what I need.

There are different kinds of letting go, but every relationship requires at least one form. Ironically, *acceptance* is sometimes the means of relinquishment. In 1980 my mother, aunt, and maternal grandmother all died. My mother fought cancer for several long months before she lost the battle at age fifty-four. In desperate hope I longed for her healing. I imagined what an inspiration it would be to my unbelieving family.

The day of my mother's death I fled the confinement of the hospital in exhaustion. Despair and doubt hurled accusations at my faith. But alone in the car on my way home, the early morning April sunrise seemed to stamp approval on my acquiescence. Weeping with my loss, I spoke out loud, "Lord, I don't understand, but I choose to believe. Even in death I will trust you."

One week later, my maternal grandmother died too. Losing her at that specific time taught me that God has a timing and purpose to our lives and deaths that may not make sense to us. Trusting his sovereignty gives hope.

As difficult as those experiences of loss were, the relinquishment of my children has been my ultimate test. My middle son, Ross, had open heart surgery at age five. The hardest part of planning his operation was that he didn't appear to need it. Offering up a healthy child to a surgeon's knife with such an intricate surgery challenged all my protective instincts. The alternative prognosis, however, was that he would have a seventy-year-old heart at age thirty. He came through completely healed. A long scar on his chest is the only visible proof of the ordeal. This year he begins his studies at Dartmouth College.

The most painful act of relinquishment for me was letting go of my eldest son in his rebellion. The same day

Ross came home to announce he had been elected president of the National Honor Society, Ryan came home to tell me he had talked to the principal about quitting school. At first, Ryan had excelled in sports and been one of the best athletes in his school without exerting much effort. But when he turned fifteen he had an identity crisis. In the middle of his eighth-grade year, we had moved to a new city where the sports programs were highly competitive and difficult to break into.

After a few rejections and what he perceived as failure, he focused his energy on playing guitar. From there he took a quick slide into darkness through rock music and drinking. Even though I had been a teenage rebel myself, I could not understand nor accept the choices Ryan was making. I had blamed my rebellion on my father's abandonment; but Ryan had loving Christian parents!

We were devastated when Ryan joined a heavy metal rock band and quit high school. He moved to the home of a friend whose parent was single and allowed more freedoms. As we reluctantly gave our permission, I'm not sure if we were letting go or giving in—I do know that his opposition to our rules and his rebellion had worn us out.

Many days I cried so hard I became physically ill. My nights were filled with fear and speculations. I knew this was beyond my control, yet I refused to let go emotionally. How could I relinquish my son to evil—maybe to his own destruction? It was one thing to let go of a son bound for college and healthy pursuits, but this? Thoughts of failure plagued me. How could my love be so impotent that he would choose this way? Why would he reject his family? There had to be something we could *do*—we were his parents!

Anxiety and fear are tormenting companions. Grief would overcome me at odd times and without warning.

Coming home from the grocery store my tears triggered an anguished lament, "Not my son, Lord—anything but this. Please, not my son."

Abruptly my moroseness was interrupted with a startling thought: "But Mary, what about *my* Son?

Caught up short by its magnitude, I almost laughed. I had to consider the implications. Yes, what about God's Son? What about Jesus? Feebly, right there in the car, I mustered a prayer offering up all of this horrendous situation to him. All my desires, all my fears, all my disappointments. I was finally willing to accept our family crisis. I opened my hands to release Ryan and his future securely into God's hands. I certainly didn't understand this trial—nor did I want it—but I chose to trust God anyway.

Even though the pain of this situation did not leave that day, the oppressive anxiety did, and with my acceptance came tremendous peace. Granted, my relinquishment was not very noble—more an act of desperation. But I've come to realize that in every act of letting go there is an element of not understanding. I think it's called trust. Otherwise, there would be no need for faith. Even so, this was not a once-for-all offering, just a beginning. But I never again experienced the oppressive anxiety I did before I was willing to accept this suffering.

The past five years have been the most difficult of my life. Even though I have seen God at work in both Ryan's life and my own, I would not choose this way to grow. But it has been the means of deepening my faith.

Frank Laubach, the great literacy missionary, says in his journal, "Having our souls made tender by some great anguish is the way God often uses for us to find his heart." My dependence on God was superficial until I trusted him with my child in the darkness. There he proved to me that his grace *is* sufficient, even in the thing I fear most. Ryan is a father himself now and is learning firsthand the liberating act of parental relinquishment.

Mary Wilken says the best part about being forty-plus is *"being a grandmother—it is grand!"* In addition to teaching Bible, Mary works in a Christian bookstore and speaks at conferences. She is the mother of Ryan, Ross, and Jeff (not to mention grandmother to Kyle) and is married to Terry Wilken, director of telephone counseling ministries for the Billy Graham Evangelistic Association.

*A bruised reed he will not
break, and a smoldering wick
he will not snuff out.*
Isaiah 42:3

God's Winter Flower

Ruth C. Lee

Bible Teacher and
Christian Dramatist
Burlington, North Carolina

"I'm so very sorry, Mrs. Lee, but you and your husband will have to choose another baby," the counselor announced.

Choose another baby! For months Allen and I, along with our seven-year-old son and five-year-old daughter, had anxiously awaited the arrival of our precious miracle from South Korea, our adopted baby daughter.

After endless pages of paperwork and hours of interviews, a four-month-old infant named Koo Yun Mee had been assigned to our family and rooted in our hearts. Our kitchen walls were decorated with world maps tracing her flight from Seoul to Los Angeles to Chicago and finally to us in Greenville, South Carolina. And now, I was barely comprehending my caller's words as she continued to relay her devastating message.

This little girl had been classified as abandoned. According to a South Korean law, she could not be released until she was at least twelve months of age, allowing adequate time to be identified by any interested party. The adoption agency's recommendation was for us to simply forget this particular child and select another child. Obviously, the probability of this child being allowed to leave the country had become very slim.

Was this call a sick joke? A bureaucratic blunder? I felt as if some unseen thug had tackled me from behind, knocking all the breath out of me. Immediately I demanded a response from God.

How dare you lead us into this decision and have us fall in love with this child only to jerk her away from our grasp! Have you suddenly changed your mind?

In the weeks that followed, the initial searing stabs of pain gave way to a numbing ache in our hearts. *Why, Lord, why? You know that we cannot select another baby. We believed that you had so carefully chosen this special one for us. What are we to do?*

"Be still and know that I am God. Obey me. Put your hope in Me."

Obey you? Even to the point of releasing this child, Lord? I cried.

My husband began to write letters to friends and to pursue any avenues leading to the release of Koo Yun Mee. But to me he simply said, "Seek God and pray."

But I couldn't pray anymore. I could only retreat within myself with sighs too deep for words. And so God came to me like a warm woolen blanket engulfing my cold heart. God wrapped me in the promises of Psalm 139: "Search me, O God, and know my heart. . . . If I go up to the heavens you are there; if I make my bed in the depths, you are there."

And I was finally able to respond: *Ready me for your will, Lord, even by breaking my own will.*

Gently God reminded me of Isaiah 42:3, "A bruised reed he will not break, and a smoldering wick he will not snuff out." Essentially God reminded me, "I am your hope . . . not the government, not the agency, only me." Romans 8:24-25 says, "But hope that is seen is no hope at all. Who hopes for what he already has? But if we hope for what we do not yet have, we wait for it patiently."

You love me unconditionally. Am I to love you with the same love? Am I to trust you, who created families, to complete my own?

Reassured by God's truths, I began to be less affected by the world's words. I often felt like a bruised reed or a dimly burning wick—bending, but not breaking; smoldering, but not snuffed out. Still uncertain of the outcome, I was sure that God was specifically teaching me to hope in him. Period.

Koo Yun Mee had been born on October 18, 1985 at a hospital in Inchon City, only to be quickly abandoned, nameless and helpless. I had envisioned a memorable Christmas with our daughter. Long winter nights to follow, cuddling her by a cozy fire—not caring for the winter winds blowing outside of our lives. But God envisioned a different, deeper journey during those winter months. A journey that would lead me around an unfamiliar bend in the road—one of complete obedience and submission and renewed hope. This winter path proved less desired and less traveled, yet well-worn by God's faithful.

Anna Hope Lee, our own Koo Yun Mee, came home to us in the spring of 1986, after that difficult winter. She arrived at just the precise moment created by God for her introduction to us. She embraced us with her faith in us with no assurance whatsoever of our love for her. She loved us immediately as she unconditionally clung to our hearts.

And she lay at our feet her dearest gift—her own evidence of God's promise of her to us in her name. *Koo Yun Mee* in Korean means "flower that blooms in winter."

Oh, God. Forgive me. Did I not see that you were lovingly nurturing and feeding our child, bringing her to full bloom? You had mercifully pruned and prepared her to travel to us. You were wisely readying us to receive her as your daughter first, and as our daughter second.

Today Anna Hope Lee is ten years old. She is so very much like the single flower surviving the icy storm, continually blooming—even in winter.

Ruth Lee says that the best part of being forty-plus is *"experiencing God's forgiveness and renewal daily."* Ruth is a graduate of Furman University and enjoys participating in drama and giving monologues. A homemaker and the mother of Abram, Jordan, and Anna, Ruth is married to Allen Lee, a certified public accountant.

Love the Lord your God
with all your heart and with
all your soul and with
all your strength. These
commandments that I give
you today are to be upon
your hearts. Impress them on
your children. Talk about them
when you sit at home and
when you walk along the road,
when you lie down and
when you get up.
Deuteronomy 6:5-7

Passing It On
Valerie Elliot Shepard

Homeschool Teacher
Trabuco Canyon, California

When are the children going to learn to sit still and listen? I inwardly whined as my husband, Walt, read the Bible during family devotions. We had tried, in fits and starts, to have our reading at the table, but there were too many distractions.

Now we go to the family room, where the distractions are who gets to sit by Mama or "Jim's bothering me!" When Walt asks a question about the Scripture, Colleen or Evangeline sheepishly give him a blank look and the older ones sigh in disgust. But, at *least* the Word of God is being read!

I never dreamed that having family devotions with our eight children would be such a challenge! After all, didn't I have a rich heritage? My uncle Bert had once remarked, "While the Howards [my mother's family] had their family Bible reading in the parlor, we Elliots [my father's family] were having ours amongst the crumbs at the breakfast table."

Now, every Saturday morning Walt and I go out for coffee to talk and pray and sometimes discuss the whole challenge of family devotions. Our conclusion is that we desperately need God's intervention into our children's hearts and that in our own strength we are failures.

But I've also recently discovered that having a family who loves the Bible, children who are always obedient, and an orderly routine had become idols in my life. Although these are all good things to strive for, God showed me that I had begun to love those things more than I loved him. I wanted to be able to say that I served these idols without fault, but because they were terribly hard taskmasters, I continually felt that I had failed. When God exposed my sin, I saw how much I had wanted to own my family and pride myself in my own works.

On this clear and cool day, I sit in my bedroom and see my failures and works everywhere. The sewing table has a pile of unmended clothes, the notions basket has been pawed through by my fourteen-month-old daughter, Sarah. But can I receive this little inconvenience as from God's hand and rejoice in the gift of this precious child? How we love to see her growing in understanding and obedience. How we all love to hold her and laugh with her. The laundry room may be messy and the kitchen floor may be dirty, but not long from now I will have plenty of time to clean; what my children need now is my love and attention.

Some mornings I feel like sending all of my children off to school because I feel inadequate as a homeschooler, but God is showing me that even though my limitations seem to make me a failure, I cannot live listening to my feelings. Even though all I may see now is disorderliness, sporadic routines, and wayward habits, God wants me to walk by faith—not by sight. I must live, instead, by his Word given to me by the quiet whisperings of his Spirit. He asks me to see my idols for what they really are. Then he shows me that *he* owns this wonderful family.

Has my trust been in *myself*—the girl who had a perfect childhood, wonderful parents, and a solid Christian heritage? For many years that is how I lived. While most people were saying they couldn't change because they were victimized during childhood, I was saying to myself, "I ought to be a perfect mother because I had such a secure and wise upbringing."

But that kind of thinking led me to depend on myself alone and not on the work of Christ. Now my weaknesses—instead of paralyzing me—are enabling me to run to Christ! My Father's strength is made perfect in my weakness. So now I run to him, begging for mercy, at every failed attempt to be perfect.

God is teaching me to look at the messy laundry room or dirty kitchen floor and be thankful for the ones he has given me to serve. He has given me—by his grace alone—eight healthy, intelligent children, a husband who loves me and is crazy about his family, a lovely home, a church we love, and a neighborhood where we long to show the love of Christ.

The Howards, the Elliots, and the Shepards all have believed in the One whose grace is greater than all our sin. May I give you the verses that have saved me from despair when I wanted to concentrate on my failures instead of his love?

And God is able to make all grace abound to you, so that in all things at all times, having all that you need, you will abound in every good work. As it is written, "He has scattered abroad his gifts to the poor; his righteousness endures forever." Now he who supplies seed to the sower and bread for food will also supply and increase your store of seed and will enlarge the harvest of your righteousness. You will be made rich in every way so that you can be generous on every occasion, and through us your generosity will result in thanksgiving to God. (2 Cor. 9:8-11)

How thankful I am to be God's child, to know that he will be faithful to this generation as he has been faithful to my ancestors before me!

Val Shepard says the best part of being forty-plus is *"seeing how God has led me so far and rejoicing in his presence for forty years!"* Val spent her early years with her mother, Elisabeth Elliot, living in the jungles of Ecuador with the Auca Indians, the tribe who had killed her missionary father, Jim Elliot. She is a graduate of Wheaton College and has homeschooled her eight children: Walter, Elisabeth, Christiana, Jim, Colleen, Evangeline, Theo, and Sarah. In addition to her ministry of hospitality, Val is also a busy clergy wife. Her husband, Walt Shepard, Jr., pastors the Aliso Creek Presbyterian Church.

About the Author

Lucinda Secrest McDowell is a dynamic speaker and the author of *Amazed By Grace* (Broadman and Holman, 1996). She has also published in more than fifty magazines and written contributing articles for three other books, *The Strength of a Woman* (Broadman and Holman Publishers, 1993), *Shaped by God's Love* (Grason, 1990), and *Stepping Out—A Guide To Short-Term Missions* (YWAM Publishing, 1992). In 1993 she was named "Writer of the Year" at the Mt. Hermon Christian Writers Conference in California.

Cindy holds degrees from Gordon-Conwell Theological Seminary and Furman University and has studied at the Wheaton Graduate School of Communication. Her background includes work as a journalist, missions director, and radio broadcaster. Currently she directs the Caring Ministries program at the First Church of Christ Congregational in Wethersfield, Connecticut.

Cindy is married to Michael and is the mother of Justin, Timothy, Fiona, and Margaret.

She would love to hear from you. Please write her at:

Encouraging Words!
P.O. Box 290707
Wethersfield, CT 06129-0707